CENTAUR PRESS
London

First published in 1999 by Centaur Press
an imprint of Open Gate Press
51 Achilles Road, London NW6 1DZ

British Library Cataloguing-in-Publication Programme
A catalogue reference for this book is available from the
British Library.

ISBN: 0 900001 43 7

The pictures on pages ii, 6, 26, 103, 108, 116, 119, 126 and 130
are © D J Wheadon and reproduced by kind permission.

The pictures on pages 12, 21 and 75 are from the
Ferne Animal Sanctuary booklet produced while
John Bryant was manager there.

The pictures on pages 109 and 146 are reproduced
by kind permission of Helen Day.

The cover photograph of Rufus the fox is reproduced
by kind permission of Gary Treadwell.

Printed in Great Britain by
The Cromwell Press, Trowbridge, Wiltshire

*To the staff and volunteers who contributed to
the caring spirit of the Ferne Animal Sanctuary
from 1976 to 1983, and to Teresa, who didn't
enter my life until many years later, but without
whose support and assistance this story would
never have been written.*

Contents

Introduction

On 1st January 1976, while most folk were still enjoying the last hours of the Christmas holiday, Sue and I (she was later to become my wife – and ex-wife!) were starting our first day managing the Ferne Animal Sanctuary. There are many animal shelters and sanctuaries in Britain, but none have a more remarkable or traumatic history than Ferne.

It all began with the outbreak of war in 1939 when Nina, the late Duchess of Hamilton and Brandon broadcast a radio message from London, in which she offered her vast stately home and Ferne estate near the village of Berwick St John in Wiltshire as a temporary refuge to pets whose owners wished to join the armed forces to fight Hitler's Germany. Returning to her Regent's Park home after the broadcast, the Duchess was shocked to find a queue of dozens of people with their cats and dogs already waiting for her.

From then on and throughout the war, special caravans packed with cats and dogs regularly made their way from London to the Duchess's mansion and rolling meadows of Ferne. Later, in the same generous and compassionate spirit, the Duchess opened up her home as a war nursery for young children blitzed out of London and other major cities.

When hostilities ceased six long years later, the children returned to their families and communities, but many pets were unclaimed; the Ferne Animal Sanctuary had begun its journey into the annals of British animal welfare history. Since then thousands of homeless and ill-treated creatures, both domestic and wild, have become members of the huge 'Ferne Family' – some of the first being nine Shire horses made redundant by Paddington Council in 1947.

The Duchess died in 1951 and death duties forced the Hamilton

Sue and I in the early days at Ferne

family to sell the Ferne estate complete with its mansion and cottages, farm buildings, gardens, woods, ponds and rich pastures.

Salvation came in the form of the Duchess's fellow anti-vivisection campaigner and fellow member of the Animal Defence Society, Miss Lind-af-Hageby. To save the sanctuary, Miss Lind stepped in and bought the entire property, but there was not enough money to maintain it in its former glory and the estate began to fall into a state of neglect – except for the facilities needed for the animals and the staff. Tragedy struck again when Miss Lind died suddenly – intestate – and ownership of the estate became an issue of a bitter legal dispute.

Eventually the court ruled that the estate was owned by the Animal Defence Society of which both Miss Lind and the Duchess had been prominent members. However, the court also ruled that the Ferne Animal Sanctuary should be regarded as a separate independent body which was occupying the estate without any rights of ownership.

Then, as is common in the world of animal welfare, internecine war broke out, and the Animal Defence Society ordered the Ferne Animal Sanctuary to vacate the estate. The Society also ordered the destruction of the mansion and its sale as scrap (it was said locally that the scrap merchant became a millionaire out of the deal) and the estate and its lovely workers' cottages, gardens, and buildings fell into terminal decline. The Trustees of the Sanctuary began to face up to eviction by running down its animal rescue work and searching for another suitable home.

In 1975, a new site for the Ferne Animal Sanctuary was purchased, a 36 acre farm formerly known as 'Downlands' on the Somerset border near Chard. The last remnants of the Duchess's sanctuary – seven horses, sixteen cats and a single donkey were loaded into lorries for transportation to their new permanent refuge and the struggle began to build anew the Duchess's concept of a sanctuary where animals could live in peace and security – where battered and tormented bodies and spirit could be revived and renewed.

That was the moment Sue and I became part of the sanctuary story. We were invited to take over the management by the Ferne trustees led by Lady Muriel Dowding, staunch anti-vivisection campaigner, founder of Beauty Without Cruelty and widow of battle of Britain hero Lord Hugh Dowding (former Air Chief Marshal). We accepted the challenge with enthusiasm and threw ourselves into the restoration of the Ferne Animal Sanctuary.

Seven years later I left – in a state of physical and emotional exhaustion. Sue had gone months earlier – our marriage shattered. Animal welfare, particularly the animal rescue part of it, is a tough and stressful business. But Sue and I, both now with new partners, can look back with some pride to several years of recreating the magic of Ferne. We raised the animal population from 24 to more than two hundred at any one time. We designed and built new kennels and stables and revamped the cattery. We incorporated natural healing methods and managed the sanctuary as the Duchess wished, on animal rights principles – that is treating each and every animal and bird as an individual, and encouraging the kinship of all human and sentient animal life.

This book is a celebration of Ferne, the creatures which found refuge within its boundary, the young staff and volunteers who gave part of their lives to the creation of Ferne's oasis of compassion, and the many visitors who found inspiration and encouragement in Ferne's unique atmosphere.

The Ferne Animal Sanctuary still exists, it still rescues animals and provides them with a secure future. It may no longer be managed in 'our way', but I hope that by recording the stories, some sad, some happy, some funny, which made our years at the sanctuary worthwhile, I can in a small way perhaps enhance what is great about the story of the Ferne Animal Sanctuary and diminish that which is not.

Donkeys

The first character we met at Ferne was Mokey, a seven-year old donkey. We had been warned by the outgoing manager that Mokey was lethal with both teeth and back feet and that he should be kept away from other animals.

What nonsense! No herd animal should ever be kept alone and so the first action we took was to open the gate of Mokey's paddock and give him the freedom of the sanctuary's 36 acres.

It was true that as far as other donkeys and horses were concerned Mokey was a loner, but he enjoyed the company of the goats, was as soppy as a puppy with children, and possessed a wicked sense of humour. He had a very thick, grey coat and he hated being groomed. When we first tried to drag a comb through his coat, he bucked, twisted, turned, lunged and indulged in a host of contortions rather than succumb. It was weeks before he twigged that not only could he get a few polo mints if he behaved, but that he also felt a lot better when all his matted and dead hair was raked out.

Mokey always had an eye open for mischief. One day, our handy-man Peter, decided to repair a crumbling section of the stone wall around Mokey's old paddock. He began by removing the loose stones, watched with great interest by Mokey and his new friends Moss and Dock, two billy-goat kids. Peter mixed a bucket of cement and then went to the tap in the yard to fill another bucket with water. When he returned to the wall he found Moss and Dock trying to eat the cement. He chased them off to the other side of the paddock and waited until they were fully occupied browsing a hedge. Returning again to his task, Peter discovered that Mokey had drunk his entire bucket of water. It was a very hot day and

Left to right: Dock, Moss and Mokey became good friends

cursing under his breath, Peter pulled off his sweater, hung it over the wall and walked back to the yard to refill his bucket. As he stood at the tap he turned just in time to see Mokey snatch his sweater from the wall and gallop off with it firmly clenched in his teeth, whirling and bucking with pure pleasure. Peter set off in pursuit, but this only heightened Mokey's fun. Every time Peter got near, Mokey spun and trotted further away – the trophy still hanging from his teeth.

Peter, by now sweating streams and puffing hard, surmised that if he stopped chasing, Mokey would tire of the game and drop the sweater. So he returned to his work, watching Mokey out of the corner of his eye, pretending to ignore him. Mokey trotted closer, swinging the piece of clothing like a bull-fighter teasing a bull – ready to leap away and continue the game if Peter made a lunge for his garment. But Peter refused to oblige and Monkey wandered off. As Peter watched, Mokey did at last drop the sweater – but only into a wet muddy patch, and to humiliate Peter even more, sank to his knees, rolled over onto his back, pressing the cloth deep into the mud. He then stumbled to his feet, shook himself and wandered off to find something less boring to do, leaving Peter to retrieve the sad looking garment from the mud-patch.

It was all too much for Peter. He abandoned the wall, retreated to the garage and spent the rest of the day tinkering with the tractor – no doubt muttering under his breath about all the nasty things he would like to do to donkeys!

We took in several donkeys over the next twelve months until we had accumulated a small herd of seven. The first was Barny, a young black and white donkey rescued by the famous Donkey Sanctuary which was sited at Sidmouth only a few miles from Ferne. The Donkey Sanctuary normally re-homed their rescued donkeys in compatible pairs, but after we explained that we were looking for a friend for Mokey, it was agreed that Barny, who had not yet been paired up, could come to Ferne.

He was only about two years old, in superb condition, extremely friendly – that is, to everybody except Mokey! The two of them completely ignored each other. They never even sniffed noses. Now we had two lonely donkeys. Two weeks later, in came two more donkeys, mother and daughter, Tina and Lucy. They had spent years neglected, hobbled together by a chain to stop them wandering from an unfenced field. The result was that they both suffered from painful, overgrown and distorted hooves, which needed the regular attention of an experienced farrier to begin the long process of reversing the deformities.

Barny instantly joined Tina and Lucy, as did the next arrival Roly, who being a dangerous kicker saved himself years of miserable toil as a beach donkey.

Still Mokey remained aloof from the growing herd of donkeys. We adopted another from the Sidmouth Donkey Sanctuary – a quiet young female, Clover. Again Mokey was not impressed and preferred the company of the goats.

But then came Joby. 'I've got this donkey,' said a voice on the phone. 'I bought him two years ago for £80 as a pet for my daughter, but the local kids keep breaking down the fence and he's always getting out.'

I asked the caller the donkey's age and was told that he was purchased at ten years old according to the previous owner. 'And who was the previous owner?' I asked, inwardly groaning at the answer – a notorious operator of beach donkeys at a famous West Country holiday resort – a man who might as well be the devil himself as far as anyone in animal welfare was concerned, particularly anyone involved in donkey rescue.

We agreed to accept the donkey and a few days later, a small horse-box towed by a car arrived at the sanctuary. I opened up the box and peered inside. At first I thought it was empty, but then saw what appeared to be a grey bundle on the floor. It looked like an old grey blanket draped over a bicycle. I shouted for Sue and climbed in. There was Joby. Not a lively twelve-year-old donkey, but a toothless, broken wreck of a beast; at least 50 years old, coated with lice and a few tufts of dry grey hair.

I thought he was dead, but as I touched his head, his huge black eyes opened and he began to struggle to rise. But he was too weak. Leaving Sue to stay with him and stop him struggling, I called a couple of builders who were working on repairs to our barn and asked them give me a hand putting down a bed of clean straw in a spare room in the house. Then with their help we physically lifted Joby out of the horse-box and carried him across the yard into the house and his bed of straw. We were all choked up with emotion and tight-lipped with anger at the appalling state of the frail old donkey. I thought he would be dead within hours. The hour's journey had clearly exhausted Joby's already desperately low physical reserves. Meanwhile Joby's owner had driven off at speed – a very wise action in the circumstances!

Then began the long struggle to restore health to an animal that had literally spent donkey's years slaving on the beach summer after summer for decade after decade with his fellow beasts of burden, wandering endlessly up and down, patiently carrying generations of excited children in the heat of the sun, an electric goad always on hand to prod him on when his old legs became tired.

Even worse, when winter came, instead of enjoying a rest with good food and a warm stable, Joby and his fellows were turned out onto a local rubbish tip to scrounge a living as best they could. They had no shelter from the winter rain and snow and only irregular feeds of mouldy hay thrown over the fence by their owner to supplement whatever they could scavenge amongst the rubbish.

The sickening thing about this notorious man was the public relations skill he deployed with the local press who regularly featured him as a popular local character cuddling the latest baby donkey born into his 'care'. For years the Donkey Sanctuary's inspectors had waited to catch him breaking the law, but he always managed to avoid prosecution through a combination of deviousness and a knowledge of the inadequacy of animal welfare legislation. He had also cultivated the friendship of several local Councillors who were always quick to defend his seedy operation.

We contacted Joby's owner (who apologised profusely for 'having to dash off' the day he delivered Joby to us) and pointed out to him that he had paid £80 for a donkey which was approaching 50 years old – not a ten year old as he had been told by the previous owner. He was shocked, but said that the transaction was for cash, at the previous owner's insistence, and there was nothing in writing to prove the fraud.

Our task now was to save Joby from further suffering and if possible give him a final year or two of peace, security, and pleasure. Firstly, we had to shave all the lice and lice-eggs from his skin after powdering him with a safe herbal insecticide. Then, despite the fact that he was indoors, we had to keep him covered with a blanket and feed him small regular meals of high-protein cereal and sweet herb-filled meadow hay. At first he was too weak to stand and to help with his circulation and to prevent fluid accumulating in his lungs, we had to turn him over every couple of hours day and night. That meant of course taking it in turns to sleep with him ... and his lice!

While he had company he was quite content, munching hay and listening to the radio. But he hated being alone and would attempt to rise as soon as his 'minder' left the room. After three weeks, and with a little help, Joby was strong enough to take a gentle stroll out through the French windows and into the orchard. He was still bald and had to wear a colourful patchwork coat knitted by sanctuary supporters. At that time, we were asked to take in five rescued battery hens – almost as bald as Joby after their year crammed in tiny cages. Such birds cannot cope with space when first taken from their cages – and certainly cannot be allowed outside. After a few days on the floor boxed into the corner of a stable, and with the boxes gradually moved outwards to provide more a little more each day, they were soon happily scratching around. So we put them in with Joby! He quite liked their company and at night they would all sit along his back to roost. It was a strange sight: five virtually bald hens all in a row, dozing on the back of an equally bald, sleeping donkey.

As he grew stronger, and we got to know him better, we remained puzzled at the old scars on his front knees and shins. It was not until much later when he was strong and he was out in our fields, that we found the answer to the mysterious damage. A donkey, like a horse, rises from lying down, by firstly standing on its front legs, and then pushing itself up into a standing position using the power of its hind legs. However, for years, Joby had been too debilitated to rise this way and had instead learned to push his back end up first until he was kneeling on his front knees, and then with a mighty effort throwing his front end upwards and scrambling his front legs into a standing position. This is how his little front knees and shins had sustained such damage, but not the only way!

We also discovered that Joby had learned some ingenious survival tactics all those years on his winter rubbish dump. He had learned to get down on his knees and scrabble under wire fences, a strategy which no doubt enabled him to find extra food. It was this trick and Joby's indomitable spirit which were to cause us many troubles over the next couple of years.

One morning, bright and early, I was out checking the horses and donkeys. They were all present and correct – except for Joby. I searched everywhere; in the field shelters and each of our eight fields, until there was only one place to look – the spinney. This was about an acre or so of scrubby woodland and undergrowth growing on a treacherous bog. It was a dangerous place for large animals and we had erected a double row of barbed wire fencing around the spinney to keep them out. We had at one time contemplated draining it, but it was a valuable habitat for a wide range of wetland fauna and flora as well as forming a corridor between blocks of woodland for foxes and roe deer.

As I walked along next to the double fence, my blood chilled when I spotted a tuft of grey hair on a barb of the bottom strand of wire. Sure enough, Joby had crawled under the fence and into the spinney. I climbed the fence and followed his hoof prints into the trees and suddenly there he was – just his head, neck and grey back protruding from the black ooze into which he had stumbled. Already up my knees in the smelly swamp I realised there was nothing I could do. He was not struggling, appeared perfectly calm and just surveyed me with his big black eyes. I ran the three hundred yards or so to the house and alerted the staff. Sue grabbed a net full of hay and ran down to the spinney while I did the only thing I could think of, and rang the fire-brigade!

Having relayed Joby's predicament over the phone to the fire station. I ran back to the spinney where Sue was crouching on a dry patch watching Joby contentedly munching hay from the net Sue had placed by his nose. Despite being stuck fast in cold, stinking mud from which there was no way he could extricate himself, he appeared totally unconcerned.

Within minutes we could hear the fire-engine siren wailing its way along the narrow country roads towards us. We had left staff in the main yard to open field gates and direct the appliance to the spinney. Soon the huge red machine came careering across the field, clattering and bouncing on the undulating pasture. Thundering along behind, tossing their heads and kicking out with their hind feet in excitement were nine horses and five other donkeys, followed by half a dozen equally excited yapping dogs. In the next paddock the goats bounced about having mock battles and our two huge pigs, Kinky and Fred, dashed up and down the fence, ears aloft, piggy-eyes blinking, snorting in disbelief at the chaotic disruption of the normally tranquil Ferne morning.

The fire-fighters were magnificent. They quickly assessed the situation, discarded their coats and waded into the mire. They dug away some of the clinging mud from Joby's flanks and while he happily continued to munch his hay, they pushed the ends of two fire-hoses down through the mud under his belly and after fishing for the ends pulled them up the other side. Then six burly fire-fighters heaved on the hoses until slowly, the slurping, squelching bog reluctantly released its victim. They carried Joby bodily into the field where we set about rubbing him down with what was left of his hay, until his circulation and feeling was restored to his skinny little legs.

Within ten minutes, the fire-fighters had scraped the worst of the mud off their boots and trousers and rewound their hoses, and Joby, having fully recovered, was casually wandering off as if nothing had happened. He only waited long enough to have his photograph taken by a local reporter who had heard the siren and followed the fire-engine from Chard.

It was not the last time Joby got into serious trouble. I glanced out of the kitchen window one day and was horrified to see him

Joby after his rescue by firefighters

tottering and stumbling along the top of a stone wall. Like an old man he was fine pottering about on a flat surface, but if he tripped, even over a small obstacle, he would go down like a sack of potatoes – and here he was bumbling along the top of an uneven wall from which there was a four feet drop onto a concrete track. I watched, my heart in my mouth, just praying that he would get to the end from which he could step onto an earth bank. But no, he tripped. staggered and dropped with a sickening thud onto the concrete. Yelling for help I raced across the yard to Joby's prone body. As Sue and others joined me, I said, 'He's gone.' There was not a flicker of life. His eyes were closed and he was not breathing. But then, as Sue was feeling for a pulse, his mouth opened and with a terrible rasping sound he dragged in a huge lung-full of air, paused for a long moment, and then gasped it out again. Another long pause which seemed ages, was followed by a second rasping breath and exhalation, and his long grey eyelashes flickered open. He was back with us. A few minutes later we had him back on his feet and he was on his way back to the fields.

It was about this time that we noticed that Mokey, who as mentioned earlier refused to mix with other donkeys, was beginning to follow Joby around. In fact, from then on, he was rarely more than a few feet from Joby. If Joby was grazing, so was Mokey. When Joby rested or slept, Mokey rested or slept next to him. And if for any reason they became separated, Mokey would bray inconsolably until they were reunited. Not that Joby showed the slightest interest in Mokey. There was absolutely no sign of Mokey's adoration being reciprocated, but until the end of Joby's life two years later, Mokey was his constant shadow. When Joby's weakness and inability to rise under his own effort was on the verge of making his life miserable and he was beginning to look thin and tired, we decided it was time for us to ease him out of his long and hard life. As he munched on his favourite treat of mashed apples, our vet slipped a needle into a vein in his neck, and he passed away.

Our practice with all deaths amongst our herd animals was to allow their kin access to the body for twenty-four hours – so they could realise that their colleague was no longer part of the herd. In Joby's case, Mokey stood silently by him, refusing to eat and drink for a full two days before his mourning was over. Then Mokey returned to his previous lifestyle, wandering Ferne with the goats and sheep. More donkeys came to Ferne, but Mokey showed no interest in any of them. We shall never know just what it was about old Joby that touched Mokey so. However, don't for one moment think that Mokey became a sad and lonely character. He lost none of his sense of mischief and delighted in sneaking up behind unsuspecting members of staff to run off with a bucket or grab a coat-tail or sleeve between his teeth for a tug-o-war. Indeed Mokey was responsible for my most embarrassing and humiliating moment. A group of school children was visiting one day and I was telling them about Mokey, who as usual was hanging around because he loved youngsters. To illustrate Mokey's sense of fun I shook the end of a towel at him to try and get him to grab it for a game of 'tug'. He firstly seemed reluctant, but when I persisted, he suddenly reached past the towel and clamped his teeth on my thumb – and refused to let go. The pain was absolutely excruciating and he just glared at me in triumph as I slowly sunk to my knees in front of him and the children fell about in hysterics. As he finally released my crushed thumb, I knew (and he seemed to know too) that with young children present I couldn't even scream an expletive at him for relief. All I could do was walk, as dignified as possible, to the water tap in the yard and hold my bruised and throbbing thumb under the ice-cold water for as long as I decently could without seeming to be too great a wimp in front of the children.

Pigs

The founder of Ferne, Nina, the Duchess of Hamilton, was a vegetarian – at a time when vegetarians were much more uncommon than today. In the Duchess's day it took considerable commitment for someone who cared about the suffering and death of animals to find an acceptable alternative diet.

The Duchess was in a difficult position. She was required, as a major landowner, to assist the 'war effort' by rearing livestock for food and she did not shirk her duty to the nation. But she insisted that animals reared on her land would be treated with compassion and respect, and receive a painless and stress-free death. The Duchess built a huge 'cow court' where her dairy herd could shelter both from winter's the rain and cold and summer's heat and flies. She also built a maternity unit so that cows could suckle their precious calves a couple of times a day – with only surplus milk being taken for human consumption.

To save her animals from the trauma of transportation and rough handling at slaughter-houses, the Duchess had a 'model slaughter-house' built at her farm on the old Ferne estate. How different from these days, more than five decades later, when calves are wrenched from their distressed mothers only hours after birth, manhandled and prodded into lorries, hawked around livestock markets, or worse, transported to foreign veal-rearing systems which are outlawed in Britain on grounds of cruelty. And how different from modern times where even the Government's own Farm Animal Welfare Council slams our standards of slaughter as cruel.

We were determined to ensure that the Duchess's philosophies were reflected in our management of the modern Ferne, and particularly with respect to any farm animals which came to the sanctuary. We also intended to allow visiting members of the public, particularly children, to have contact with any cows, sheep, pigs and poultry, which most people never touch until they take their packaged flesh from a supermarket shelf.

Of all farm animals, none have a worse time than pigs. These highly gregarious and intelligent animals often spend their whole lives in sheds on concrete or metal grids, with no little or no bedding, and never having the opportunity to root around in the fields with the sun on their backs. So when we were asked to take in a pig, we jumped at the chance. A local Irish girl, Eileen, had just joined our staff. Like us she was a vegetarian, but for several months she had worked in a so-called 'wildlife park'. She had resigned in disgust at some of the cruelty she had seen in the park, but before she left she managed to strike a bargain for the life of a pig called Fred, who she had looked after in the park's pets' corner. Like so many such establishments of human entertainment, the park kept a few baby animals in the pets' corner to attract and amuse children, but when the animals grew up they were 'got rid of' and replaced by more baby animals.

Fred was now five months old and had outgrown the pets' corner. The park manager had promised Eileen that Fred would not go for slaughter, provided we could take him at Ferne. Even then they insisted on us paying cash for him! Fred settled in immediately and joined our rapidly growing herd of goats. He was gentle as a lamb, loved to play – but had considerable trouble trying to get the goats to join him in his silliness.

A couple of months later, after Fred had been neutered, we purchased another 'reject' pig from the same wildlife park. Kinky was an immediate hit with Fred and from the first moment they were inseparable. We converted a shed in the goats' paddock into night-quarters for them and filled it with bales of shredded newspaper which they would busily convert into a huge cosy heap by each grabbing great mouthfuls of the packed paper and shaking it loose. On cold nights it was a real treat to peep in with a torch and see nothing but two pink snoring snouts poking out of their king-sized bed. Pigs are so clean, of course, that we only needed to change their bedding every few months. Even in driving rain they would always go outside to urinate or defaecate. Neither of them, or indeed any of the pigs we took in later, ever fouled their sleeping quarters.

The tragedy for pigs kept in modern factory farms is that they have no choice but to foul their own living and sleeping environment – such instinctively clean animals must find this distressing, but then anyone who kept a dog in the conditions millions of pigs have to endure would be branded a monster and dragged into court for cruelty!

Soon half the goats' paddock had been churned up by Fred's and Kinky's powerful snouts and consequently wherever they went they were followed by an assorted troupe of chickens and bantams eagerly snatching worms and grubs exposed by the pigs' rooting. A visiting farmer commented one day: 'thee wanna get rings put

Fred and Kinky taking a cool bath

in they pigs' noses – or they'll ruin thick field'. We scoffed at the idea of subjecting our wonderful pigs to such a painful mutilation. The fields could soon be repaired with a set of chain harrows and a roller – and anyway the fields had been purchased for the benefit of such animals, not to look nice and flat and green! The farmer looked completely baffled when I explained that the pigs would be staying at the sanctuary for life and would never change hands for money or end up being eaten by humans. As far as he was concerned pigs were not individual living creatures. They were bacon, ham or pork.

The problem with modern pigs is that they are not designed to live long lives. They have been genetically manipulated from the superb wild boar of yesteryear, to put on maximum weight in the minimum time so that they can be slaughtered at only weeks or months old – unless kept for breeding other pigs. Because of genetic weaknesses our pigs were constantly troubled by foot problems, particularly when the ground was dry and hard in summer or frosted in winter. They also had vulnerable digestive systems – we had to be careful they did not pick up anything which might upset them.

Our other great problem with the pigs, was that although we allowed animals and birds of many differing species to wander freely and mix happily together, we found that the horses would not tolerate the pigs anywhere near them. The animosity was all from the horses, and with the pigs being full of life and as curious as cats, we had to be careful to make sure that they could not get out in to the horses' fields. It was probably almost inevitable that one day tragedy struck. Fred, so friendly and trusting, managed to find his way unobserved to the stables. When he was missed, a search found him lying in one of the stables, in obvious distress and with an imprint of a hoof the size of a dinner plate on the side of his stomach.

From the size of the mark we assumed the culprit was Patrick, our 35 year old Clydesdale horse. If Patrick had kicked an animal the size of a dog with one of his massive back feet, it would have flown for yards and, apart from bruising and a scare, would have probably avoided serious injury. But such an impact on a massive and immovable adult pig would be totally absorbed into the body. We persuaded Fred to walk back to his paddock and into his shed where an anxious Kinky fussed around him while we phoned our vet. He soon arrived to examine Fred, but could only advise us to wait and see whether the injuries were more serious than bruising. We settled him down for the night covered with blankets, with Kinky in attendance. Sue and her mother, who was visiting us for a week, sat with him all night, taking his temperature every hour and trying to keep his spirits up. But it was no use. At dawn he died – a post-mortem the next day showing that a rupture of the gut and peritonitis were the cause of death.

Then our thoughts turned to Kinky. There was quite a mess after the post-mortem which, due to Fred's massive size, had been carried out where he died in his shed. After removing his body we decided to clean out the entire stable, but I had just begun work with pitch-fork, wheel-barrow and broom when Kinky came into the shed and laid down in the corner. With her head resting on her front legs she silently watched my every move. It was more than two hours before the shed was spotless and fresh bedding had been laid. Throughout that time Kinky only moved twice – to go outside to urinate – after which she returned to watch me sweep away all trace of her beloved Fred.

No amount of fussing or treats would cheer her up and two days later we realised that there was a danger of her becoming ill if she continued to pine so deeply. In desperation we rang a local supporter of the sanctuary who, although a pig farmer, kept her animals in great comfort and farmed more for a hobby than a business. We explained the problem and she immediately offered us a young boar named Laurel who was the same age as Kinky and had been the runt of a litter.

Within an hour Laurel was meeting Kinky. He was a horror! Greedy, bossy, aggressive and totally uninhibited in his new sur-roundings. He was in fact exactly what was needed to knock Kinky out of her gloom. Very quickly they were as inseparable as Kinky and Fred once were, and for many happy years they rooted up our fields, wallowed in our pond on hot summer days, and cuddled up together in their huge nest of shredded paper on cold nights. Pigs are such a pleasure to keep if one allows them a little freedom and dignity. What a shame so few of these intelligent and sensitive animals have the chance to enjoy such simple and natural pleasures.

Rasher and puppy pal

Pigs have been known to be perfectly clean house-pets. One, Rasher, came to us only because he got so large and heavy that the settee on which he slept collapsed under the strain. Rasher was the friendliest and gentlest pig of the many that came to Ferne thereafter. Pigs normally lose all control of their manners at feeding time, but Rasher would gently take a tiny titbit from one's fingers – unlike Laurel, who would swallow your whole arm given the chance!

Dogs

One of the first dogs we took in at the new Ferne was Ben, an old blind black Labrador. He came to us after being rescued from two years of imprisonment in a dark shed. Fed on little more than bread, he had suffered from malnutrition and lack of light and fresh air. He emerged grey with mange, canker dripped from his ears and his eyes were white and sightless.

In a few weeks at Ferne, with a good diet and course of cleansing herbal treatment, he was beginning to grow a new black coat. His canker was cured and he stopped scratching his ears. But there was nothing we could do about his blindness. At first we feared that if he stumbled into the hind legs of a donkey and unwittingly got within butting distance of a goat, he could be in trouble. But one of the first things we noticed at Ferne was just how sensitive animals seem to be to disabilities of other. After a few bumps he plodded happily around the yard and orchard.

Blind Ben

Ben was a great favourite with visiting school children and his tail would lash from side to side at the sound of their voices as he plodded fearlessly towards them. We had only one problem with Ben. He could smell a bitch in season miles away. Twice we had to drive the two miles to the village and collect him from farms where he was pestering a bitch in season. He got extremely adept at sneaking off without anyone noticing and although the roads around us were reasonably quiet, we feared his blindness was sure to result in some sort of accident sooner or later.

The last straw came with a phone call from a neighbouring farmer who told us that he had spotted an old black Labrador trapped in a wire fence while he was out in his fields in his tractor. When we arrived at the scene we found Ben lying down with this head halfway through a gap in the fence. The end of a broken piece of wire had pierced his jowls and he was caught like a fish on a hook, unable to move forwards or backwards. We snipped him free with wire cutters and took him home to treat his wound and have a serious discussion about his future.

It was very unlikely that he would find a home with a new owner – not many people would adopt a ten year old blind Labrador. Anyway he had only just learned his way around the sanctuary after his previous life in incarceration and it seemed unfair to expect him to learn yet another environment. It was out of the of the question to put him into the kennels as they were only for temporary housing of dogs for which we hoped to find new homes. The dogs which for one reason or another looked as if they would be with us for a long period of life, we attempted to turn into 'yardies'. They slept together in a large room in our house at night, and pottered around with the staff all day.

There was only one thing for it. Ben would have to be neutered – even though he was ten years old. We always spayed bitches before rehoming to prevent even more unwanted dogs being born into a world where thousands are destroyed every day as 'unwanted'. And we occasionally neutered a young dog if it could not be deterred from displaying sexual behaviour such as 'riding' human legs or trying to mount children. We had a chat with our vet who checked Ben over and confirmed that he was fit enough for such an operation and that there was a good chance of its solving the problem of Ben's wandering.

The operation was a complete success and for the rest of his life he wandered contentedly around the grounds and slept in the staff quarters in his own armchair. He continued to be a favourite of the visitors and greeted each child with such a show of affection that I became convinced that buried in his memory was a childhood friend who played with him before the long, silent, dark days he spent locked up in his gloomy prison.

Eventually Ben became incontinent, which greatly distressed him. Despite his background he was always perfectly clean in our house and in the staff bungalow. He would just stand silently at the door if he needed to go out. Nobody minded him being incontinent, of course, but when he realised he had made a puddle, his ears went down and he thrust his tail between his legs and we would have to make a fuss of him and get his tail waving again. But as his incontinence worsened, so did his distress and finally we called out our vet who, after an examination, agreed with us that it was time Ben was relieved of his burden. As he dozed happily in his favourite armchair, our vet slipped a dose of barbiturate into his vein and he was gone.

At least he had a few happy twilight years and a totally pain-free death. But nothing we could do could have ever made up for the two years of misery inflicted on him by someone claiming to be a human being.

Yet another example of man's callousness is the story of 'Ermine' or 'Min' as we called her. She began life in the window of a London pet shop where she was noticed by a passing supporter of the Ferne Animal Sanctuary. She thought the tiny eight-week old white mongrel puppy looked a little odd and when she anxiously entered the shop for a closer look, she saw immediately that the albino puppy was completely blind. An argument with the shop owner ensued and only ended when the brave lady was permitted to leave with the puppy.

That was how Ermine came to Ferne, where we quickly discovered that she was not only blind, but was also stone-deaf. The fact that such a handicapped puppy was on sale in a pet shop window, is surely an indictment of selling pets as if they were fluffy toys. Displayed in windows they are always liable to be bought on impulse and therefore more likely to be discarded when the idea turns out to be not so good after all.

When we realised the full extent of Min's disabilities we had a serious debate on whether she was capable of living a reasonable life, particularly at Ferne surrounded by horses, pigs, goats, dogs and a host of other hazards and obstacles. But we need not have worried. Min was the happiest animal I have ever known in my life. From day one she joined in rough-and-tumbles with other puppies, shrieked in excitement at a touch by a human being and, after quickly learning her way around the large lawned orchard, she would run like the wind from one end to another with complete confidence.

She would spend hours amusing herself with nothing more than a hole she had dug in the lawn, or launching mock attacks on a tree stump. Her directional instincts were uncanny and her greatest delight was sneaking up on a group of bantams scratching around on the lawn and suddenly dashing at them, scattering them squawking in all directions. Although she could see and hear nothing she seemed fully aware of the brief panic she could create in silly bantams! Such regular 'attacks' never persuaded the birds to abandon the garden, even though they had 36 acres to roam in.

At night Min was always totally exhausted. She slept in her own basket in the large room with the other ten or so 'yardies' – the dogs which through age or disability were unlikely to find a new home of their own. All around the room were dog-baskets, mostly battered and well-chewed, filled with shredded newspaper. One or other of us would go quietly into the room at night to check they were all settled, to top up their bucket of water, and offer a few reassuring words and a pat on the head to a fretting newcomer. When we entered the room, one or two dogs would yawn and stretch, a tail or two would wag and occasionally a dog would pad across for a cuddle. But Min was oblivious! She would be on her back, all four feet in the air, with her head hanging over the edge of the basket. It was fatal to lay a hand on her. One touch and she would be instantly awake, spining like a top, yapping and yiking hysterically, crashing into baskets, shattering the sleep of the other dogs, and blissfully unaware of the snarls and growls she provoked.

Nothing seemed to get her down. Visitors' day was her special treat. People just couldn't resist her and she was crazy about children, often knocking toddlers flat as she jumped up to lick their faces. People would stand and stare in amazement as she streaked around the orchard, running at full speed, magically missing trees and other obstacles. Even when she made a mistake

24

and careered into a passing dog or a wheel-barrow left in her way, she would only pause for a second with her ears momentarily dropped, before reassured, she would hurtle off again barking shrilly with the joy of living.

We never regretted for one moment our decision to accept her at the sanctuary. Many animal homes confronted with a deaf and blind puppy would have humanely destroyed it without hesitation 'to save it further suffering'. But, anyone who has ever met Min would reject such a suggestion. Well, all except one lady who arrived one Sunday afternoon to look around the sanctuary. We had a car park at the main gate where we asked visitors to leave their cars rather than drive down the steep track to the centre. There were always animals and birds wandering around on the track and in the yard, which was anyway too small to use as a car park. However, on this particular Sunday, a lady walked down the track and asked if we minded if she drove her car down as her elderly mother was a bit weak on her legs and couldn't manage the walk down the rough track. We agreed, of course, and made sure that the track and yard were clear of animals. The old (and very crotchety) lady joined us as I was showing a small group of people around. Progress was slow as the old lady, mumbling and grumbling, was aided by a walking stick and her daughter supporting her arm. We entered the orchard and there was Min sitting in the sun on the step to the dogs' room. As Min's tail flickered as her keen nose began to sense our presence, I explained about her albinoism and disabilities, and then reached forward and touched her head. As usual she erupted into life, dancing on her hind legs amongst the visitors, barking with ecstasy. Everyone was captivated. Then she whirled, sped through a gateway out of the yard and into the orchard, where she span a couple of times, tore to the other end, and then raced back again scattering a few chickens on the way. The visitors watched in disbelief their faces wreathed in smiles at Min's infectious joy. Then came the words of the grumpy woman. 'Blind and deaf? Ought to be put down,' she snapped. I turned and saw the embarrassment in the eyes of the others and a flash of anger welled up inside me. I heard myself say loudly, 'At least she can walk up and down the bloody drive!' I could have bitten my tongue off – after all we relied on the public for their support and in charitable circles, as in trade, the customer is always right. However, I was saved by the fact that several others laughed at my outburst and the old lady showed no reaction at all. Perhaps she didn't hear me. It was just as well.

Not all dogs which arrived at Ferne were brought in openly. One dreadfully wild, wet and windy night, Gary, our kennel-man, had what he described as a funny feeling and, acting on impulse, walked up the drive in the darkness to the main gate. To his

Gary with 'Spooky'

amazement there tied to the gate was a shaggy, brown-coated mongrel. It was almost inevitable that we named the dog Spooky and he was soon tucking into a meal in a warm kennel. Later that evening we received a telephone call from a tearful woman who informed us that she had tied her dog to our gate and implored us to look after him. She rang off before we could ask for details of the dog, its background or even its name. The problem in such cases is that it is very difficult to set about finding a new home for a dog when you can't tell prospective owners anything about the animal's past. Why was it dumped? Was it dirty or destructive in the house? Did its barking annoy the neighbours? Did it bite the postmen or savage a child?

We persuaded the local newspaper to publish Spooky's story with his picture in the hope that someone would recognise him or that his ex-owner would volunteer some details. But we heard nothing. Spooky settled well into a kennel pack, but it was years before we managed to find him a new home.

Anyone involved in animal rescue will say that the dumping of dogs at shelter gates is a nightmare. No background, veterinary history and temperament problems are known, which means that all these factors have to be discovered while the animal is in kennels – hardly an ideal situation because behaviour changes in kennels. And of course such dumping causes great distress to the animal itself. At a sanctuary like Ferne, miles from anywhere with no-one arriving or leaving from dusk to well after dawn, an animal could die of exposure if tied to the gate after dark.

For years it had been my ambition to catch a dog dumper in the act. Either one of the monsters who push their dog out of their car deep in the countryside or on a motorway, or one of the cowards who sneakily dump their animal and their responsibilities onto someone else. Usually such people get away with it, because even if they are seen, caring people are too busy helping the animal to chase the car and get a registration number. Well one day we did catch a dog dumper.

Sue and I had just returned from a visit to our vets in Axminster where we had dropped off a cat for neutering. As we approached our gates at about 6 pm on the summer evening, we saw a red van parked opposite the gates facing in our direction. We saw a man cross the road from our gate and get into the driver's seat. Just as we were pulling into the gateway the red van sped off past us, tyres screaming. There, inside the gate, tied to the sanctuary sign was a young black and tan mongrel. This was our chance. The dog was safe for the moment so I swung our little Renault 4 van around and we hurtled off back towards Axminster. I drove as fast as I dared along the country road, but the red van was moving at around 80 miles per hour and leaving us standing. After five miles the van was nowhere in sight, but as I came around a bend we saw two cars stopped – one almost in the hedge and both drivers just getting out of the vehicles. I pulled up and asked if a red van had passed. One of the men pointed in the direction we were travelling and said that it had almost crashed into them.

We continued our pursuit, but could not find the van which we assumed must have darted down one of the many lanes off the road. We reluctantly turned round and drove much more slowly back towards the sanctuary. As we passed the turning to Chardstock I glanced down the lane and by pure chance just caught a glimpse of a red roof of a van above the hedgerows. I slammed on the brakes, reversed and turned down the lane and within seconds we were practically breathing down the exhaust pipe of the red van. The driver was busy chatting to his female passenger and no doubt thinking he had shaken us off, did not realise we were only feet behind him.

As Sue wrote down his registration number, the driver suddenly looked in his mirror and saw us. He said something to his partner who turned her head to look at us, and moments later the red van slowed down and pulled into a farm gateway. I pulled the Renault across the front of his van to make sure he stayed where he was, and Sue and I got out. As we approached, the driver wound down his window and began to say something, but I was not going to let him spoil my triumphant moment. 'Don't bother mate,' I blasted. 'You're nicked.' A bit melodramatic I admit, but tremendously satisfying!

Neither the driver or his female partner said anything and we had nothing further to say to them. Still elated we drove back to the sanctuary to find that one of the lads, Andy, had already retrieved the dog from the entrance. He had heard the two vehicles racing off and had run up the track to investigate. After checking the dog over and finding that it seemed in reasonable condition, we rang the police and reported the incident. To my amazement the police told me that the driver had already been into the station and told them what had happened. The driver's version was that he had seen the dog tied up at the M5 interchange at Taunton and decided to rescue it and bring it to Ferne. I pointed out that the local RSPCA kennels were only four miles from the interchange and that his route must have virtually taken him past their door. Why drive a further ten miles to another animal centre? In my view he had committed two offences. Firstly, he had failed to comply with the then existing Dogs (Amendment) Act 1928 which placed a legal obligation on the finder of a stray dog to take it to the nearest police station, and secondly he had contravened the Abandonment of Animals Act 1960 by abandoning the dog in circumstances where it was likely to suffer. After all, he had dumped the dog after our closing time that was clearly displayed at the entrance and for all he knew the dog could have been tied there for fourteen hours without food, water or shelter until outside staff arrived the next morning.

I typed a full statement for the Chard police and took it to the station. I was told that they would re-type it onto the appropriate form and telephone me when it was ready for me to sign. However, when I went in they had completely re-written the statement leaving out all reference to the high-speed chase which I thought constituted guilty behaviour, and had added a line stating, 'I will support the police in whatever action they may decide to take.' I refused to sign the statement and wrote out another, but it was obvious that the police had no intention of taking any action against the driver – even though one officer confided in me that the driver had no driving licence! When I asked why no action was being taken, I was told, 'He's just a nutter, John.' So yet another dog dumper got away with it.

During my period at Ferne, we took in more than 400 dogs. Some were cruelty victims, some police strays and some simply unwanted. The late John Hughes who at that time was manager of the RSPCA kennels near Taunton, once told me that a couple had turned up one day with a nice-looking, well-behaved adult yellow

Labrador that they had owned since it was eight weeks old. The couple asked John if the RSPCA could find the dog a new home and when pressed, explained that it clashed with the colours of their new curtains and carpets!

Sometimes dogs came to us because their owners genuinely could no longer care for them. One of these rare victims of circumstances was Nicky, a small black mongrel aged eight and just beginning to show a little grey around his muzzle. He had spent his entire life as the much-loved pet of a caring, responsible family. However, the daughter in the family suffered badly from asthma and after years of investigation and various treatments, a specialists had concluded that the little girl was allergic to dog hair and advised that the family should part with Nicky.

Imagine the heartbreak of such a decision. A well-loved and loving little dog, with no vices, well adjusted – suddenly expelled from the only home and family he had ever known. The whole family came with him to hand him into our care – which we assumed would be permanent because a dog of his age was unlikely to be adopted.

The family sat in tears in our office while we completed the documents transferring Nicky's ownership to Ferne. There is not much you can say in such circumstances except to try and reassure them that Nicky would quickly settle in – as in fact almost all dogs do. They had clearly agonised over the decision for a long time and I concentrated on trying to convince them that although they would be upset for a long time, it was unlikely that Nicky would be a 'Greyfriar's Bobby', the dog which it is claimed pined to death on his master's grave, was an exception – even assuming the legend is true. Of course dogs suffer from the loss of their 'pack' and home, and it is now well-known that dogs in quarantine sometimes become so miserable and distressed that they lose condition, become ill and even die. But in my view that is because they are slammed-up in drab, concrete prisons – alone.

Many animal rescue centres still keep their stray and unwanted dogs alone in individual kennels. This isolation is totally alien to pack animals such as dogs. If a dog has to lose its pack it must be given another one – even if it is only temporary. When we built our new kennels at Ferne, we carefully designed them to comply with the requirements of wolves – the ancestors of all dogs. We had five large rooms each big enough for a small pack of four or five dogs. Down one whole side of the room was a 'dished' bed filled with shredded newspaper which was changed and burnt every week to break the life-cycles of any fleas or other parasites. For cold weather a wooden box cover could be lowered over the bed so that all the dogs could snuggle inside in the warmth of their combined body heat. There was rarely need for any other form of heating. Immediately outside each room was a small, roofed concrete pen, and adjoining that was a large grass run divided from the neighbouring run by solid wooden fencing

This design gave each pack its home 'cave' for shelter, a small dry area and a large grass pen for the pack's 'home territory'. At least once and usually twice every day, each pack was taken out into a large grass paddock of about an acre. Apart from meal times, this was the most exciting part of the day for the dogs. They would hurtle up the corridor barking with excitement out into the run, which was 'neutral territory'. They would race all round the perimeter fence, sniffing where the previous pack had been, urinating profusely to leave their own signals for the next pack. While they were in the paddock, staff would carry out any grooming, play with those which liked a game with a ball, and collect up faeces in a bucket – an unpleasant task, but necessary to keep the paddock clean and free of parasitic worms.

We also had three isolation kennels, but they were reserved for the odd inveterate fighter or whelping bitch. I never knew a dog to pine in the kennels, no matter how happy their previous home. They were far too busy finding their place in the new pecking order and there was always too much going on around them for brooding about their fate.

Nicky was even luckier. We decided that as he was unlikely to find a new home at his age and because he was such a pleasant little chap, we should make him one of the ten to a dozen 'yardies' who wandered round the sanctuary freely all day and slept together in a large room in our house at night. Nicky's family had of course been greeted by several of the 'yardies' when they arrived and although they were not at all convinced that Nicky would not pine dreadfully for them, they felt a little better seeing the sort of lifestyle he would have at Ferne. I suppose we all like to think that we are very special to our pets; it hurts our pride to think that a dog we have cared for and known for years would soon forget us, but I'm afraid, in virtually every case it is true – provided they have a new pack to join.

Nicky's family left in tears and Nicky, with his front feet on the office window-sill, whined anxiously as he watched them depart without him.

But, within minutes Nicky had made a great pal of Solo, our own black and white collie cross bitch, and they were chasing each other round the orchard. Whenever we made a trip to town for supplies or visited our vets in Axminster, Solo and Nicky always came too. Soon it was if he had been with us all his life.

One day, ten months later, a young family came to Ferne wishing to adopt a dog. They had explained on the phone that they wanted a young dog, preferably a puppy, and I had already discussed possible candidates with the kennel staff. However, when they arrived in the yard, they were greeted by Nicky. They fell for him immediately. No other dog would do, despite his age. Two days later I delivered him to his new home and left him lying on his back having his tummy rubbed by two adoring children. It was there, many years later and losing his sight and enthusiasm for life, that he died. A lucky dog was Nicky – two family homes in his life and adored in both of them.

Another lucky dog who found happiness – this time not until nearing the end of her life, was Ace, a German Shepherd. She came to us at 14 years old and had spent 12 years living in a petrol station and garage in South London as a guard dog. She spent every night of those twelve years alone, sleeping on an oily blanket on a hard concrete floor. Amazingly, and disgracefully, it was Battersea Dogs' Home that had sold her into that miserable existence. No doubt she would have eventually died knowing no other life, had it not been for the fact that she began howling at night in the garage, and in doing so upset the neighbours. The local authority received complaints and insisted that the nuisance be ended. It was then that some nearby Ferne supporters heard of her plight and stepped in to rescue her.

We thought she could become one of the 'yardies', but whilst friendly with the other dogs, she could not resist chasing the chickens – even at her age. Reluctantly we decided she would have to join one of kennel packs, but firstly we had to get twelve years of grease and oily grime out of her thick coat. This took several washes, but with a new diet supplemented by the cleansing properties of garlic, parsley and watercress, and a comfortable bed to sleep on, she soon began to look like a very fine and lively example of her breed.

We persuaded the local newspaper to tell Ace's story in the somewhat vain hope that someone would offer her a home. It worked! Within a week I was delivering Ace to the Ilminster home of a semi-retired couple. We explained that Ace had never lived in a normal home and therefore we couldn't be sure that she was house-trained or that she wouldn't chew the furniture or steal food. We needn't have worried. She settled immediately, was quiet at night and completely clean. The adaptability of dogs is amazing. Here was a dog which had probably never lived in a house, had never been taken for a walk or had played a 'game' with a human in her life. Now, at the age of fourteen, she had settled into a home, went for long country walks, played in the garden and snoozed in front of the fire as if she had lived in such an environment all her life. That is how she spent her last three years – eventually dying old and happy after giving her new owners a great deal of pleasure. How they deserved such a fine dog!

That cannot be said of every owner, and certainly not of every German Shepherd owner. It is widely accepted that all dogs originate from the wolf. It may be hard to appreciate this when looking at toy poodles, Chihuahuas and great Danes and other genetically engineered freaks, but easier when considering the looks and shape of the German Shepherd or Alsatian. It is because of the wolf's mythical reputation for ferocity, cunning and viciousness that German Shepherds are so commonly used as 'guard dogs', and by the armed forces and police for security and crowd control. In fact the wolf is a much maligned creature that has been persecuted and driven to extinction in many parts of the world on the grounds that not only is it a threat to livestock (which it clearly can be if humans slaughter the local natural prey, and destroy the forests in order to farm millions of sheep!) but also that the wolf is a hunter and killer of man. Wolves are still persecuted in Canada despite the fact that in the entire history of North America there has not been one substantiated case of a wolf attacking a human being. It is tales like Little Red Riding Hood, perpetuating a false image of wolves in the minds of successive generations, that have led to such undeserved and usually extremely cruel persecution of these magnificent animals. The bad image of the wolf has also caused much misery to German Shepherd dogs – because of their physical similarity.

The problem with the 'Rambos' who use a big dog to reinforce their image, is that they often bully and ill-treat their dogs to try and prove their manhood. One such unfortunate dog was Duke (they often have names like Sabre, Fang, King etc, in the same way as pit bull owners named their dogs after champion boxers such as Tyson and Bruno). Duke belonged to a petty criminal from Chard. This minor thug enjoyed taking Duke around the town and encouraging him to attack people. When Duke obliged, his owner would demonstrate his 'courage' and dominance over his dog by beating him with a stick until he cowered on the ground.

One day this so-called human being hit Duke once too often and one of the bystanders who was supposed to have been impressed by the display of dominion, showed his admiration by flattening Duke's owner with a punch on the nose, and taking his dog away from him.

Unfortunately this admirable chap was in no position to keep Duke. He and his wife and new baby lived in the rented lodge of a nearby stately home roamed by fashionable peacocks which were the pride and joy of the landlord. The lodge had no fenced garden and after Duke had removed a few yard-long tail feathers from a couple of the birds, his rescuer rang us for help. He warned us that Duke would attack any stranger on sight and would chase any kind of animal or bird – not exactly the sort of dog to plod around the Ferne Animal Sanctuary. But we went to have a look at him anyway. Sue could charm just about any dog, and it was not long before she was taking him for a walk along the road outside the lodge.

The trick with dogs like Duke, and particularly I find with German Shepherds, is to avoid their eyes until you have made their acquaintance and shown you are friendly. If you spend some time in your local park, where dogs are allowed off the lead, it is easy to see why there are so few fights. When dogs which are new to each other meet for the first time, they usually go immediately nose to tail with their tails wagging, and take it in turns to sniff each other's anal glands and genitals. The danger comes when two dogs meet face to face and glare at each other, stiff-legged with tails aloft and rigid. This is common when both dogs are on leads and are prevented from meeting and greeting with the canine etiquette which evolution has dictated for hundreds of thousands of years. That is when a fight is likely.

Duke waits for a game

It is the stare which is the challenge. So if you are nervous of a strange dog, of any size or type, try to avoid its eyes. Pretend that you have not even noticed it. Don't be concerned about your sweaty palms or beating heart; it is a myth that dogs smell fear or are provoked into attack by the scent of adrenaline. If the latter was true every dog within a mile of Wembley Stadium would go berserk on Cup Final day! It is physical signals to which dogs react, such as staring (challenge), running away (prey behaviour) or staring and raising the arms (imminent attack). The latter is normal behaviour for a frightened human being. It makes sense to concentrate wide-eyed at an animal you suspect is about to attack and to instinctively raise one's arms to defend the throat area. Unfortunately, to a dog, this can be wrongly interpreted as a sign that you are about to attack, and it may decide to attack first.

Duke came back to Ferne with us and we paired him with a crazy yellow Labrador named Ochre. She was only six months old and mad as a hatter. In my experience yellow Labradors are often completely scatty and boisterous until they suddenly seem to become reasonably sensible at three years old. It is hardly worth bothering to train them until then. (Just a personal view!) Before we had the new kennels built, Duke and Ochre shared a 12 feet square room with almost an acre of fenced paddock where they would run and play for hours or flop out asleep together in the sun. Apart from one short and disastrous trial in a new home, Ferne was to be Duke's home for the rest of his life. He was very special to all the staff and when the new kennels were built he became a leader of one of the kennel packs – a role in which he showed great patience and tolerance, dominating without aggression.

He loved carrying round a house-brick in his jaws – a habit

Ochre was crazy until she was three years old

which resulted in his teeth being badly worn down – and he would collect and hide dozens of sticks and stones in his bed. Once you had been introduced to Duke, he was your friend for life. He never growled at any of the many members of staff who came and went over the years, provided the procedure of introduction was strictly adhered to. When it became necessary for Duke to meet someone new, he had to be walked on the lead by someone he trusted to a field, with the new person hanging around under strict instructions not to speak to him or look him in the face. Then a stick was thrown for Duke to retrieve. Once a stick was in his mouth nothing would induce him to drop it – so one could relax!

The next step was to hand another stick to the new person while Duke was on his way back with the first one. The new person would be told to shout 'Here Duke', and throw the stick as far as possible. Duke would run and fetch sticks all day; it was his greatest joy. The trouble was, he would only pick them up; he would never put them down, and when Duke was led back to the kennel by his new friend, he would be still trying to keep eight or nine sticks clamped in his jaws. Once you had gone through this procedure you were trusted and he would do anything for you. He loved a cuddle last thing at night and would sit and 'shake a paw' for anyone he knew.

Yet any stranger coming to the kennels to look for a new dog, had only to peer through the mesh door and look at Duke and he would roar and throw himself at the door without warning. The brutal treatment meted out to him by his first owner for four years meant that Duke had to be considered a dangerous dog. But he was so loved by the staff that even after a long working day, someone would always offer to take him for a walk across the fields. He could even be let off the lead if the horses were not in sight, and after half an hour or so he would be plodding home, panting and puffing with a variety of sticks sticking out of the side of his mouth at all angles.

Duke died suddenly six years later from an unexpected and unexplained kidney collapse. Our vet fought hard to save him, but he slipped away surrounded by the entire staff of the sanctuary. No-one said much for the next few days.

By the way, throwing sticks for dogs to chase and retrieve is not really a good idea. Nasty throat injuries can occur when a dog chases after a thrown stick and tries to grab it 'end-on' as it bounces. A rubber 'stick' or ball is a safer toy.

Another German Shepherd who made a real impression on us was Holly. We first heard of her from a distressed resident of Bridgwater who told us that the young bitch had begun her street life at around 6 months of age and had been wandering housing estates for eighteen months. She survived by raiding rubbish bags and bird tables, supplemented by hand-outs from a few kindly residents, but no-one could get close enough to capture her. RSPCA Inspectors tried many times, as did the police, but they only managed to make her even more wary of human beings.

When the lady called, it was a foul, wet and cold February day. After recounting the dog's history she said that it was looking very weak and distressed and at that moment was hiding shivering under a rabbit hutch at the bottom of a neighbour's garden. Sue set off in the van to drive the 25 miles or so to Bridgwater and within three hours was back at Ferne with a bony and matted little German Shepherd bitch curled up asleep on blankets in the back of the van. Grateful Bridgwater residents acclaimed Sue as a heroine and the following week the local newspaper published the story – making much of the fact that Sue had only taken an hour to win the sad stray's confidence and slip a collar and lead on her, something the combined forces of the police and RSPCA had failed to do in eighteen months!

Holly, as Sue named her, was in a dreadful state. Her coat was thick and matted, but it hid a body of skin and bone. We settled her into a warm isolation kennel in a deep bed of shredded newspaper and the long struggle to rebuild her strength and spirit began. We organised a rota to ensure that during the day there was always someone sitting in with her to win her trust and to take her out for a few minutes walk a few times a day.

Seven days later, she totally surprised us by giving birth to seven puppies, of which three were still-born. We had suspected she might be pregnant, but in her emaciated state we had no idea she was so close to giving birth. Fortunately Sue and our kennel-maid Donna were on hand to act as midwives.

The four surviving pups seemed well except that two were born without tails! Holly was an excellent mother, but as the weeks went by we became concerned about her slow rate of recovery. Then, when the pups were a month old Holly had a bad bout of diarrhoea and collapsed. Our vet was on the spot within minutes and said he suspected parvovirus. Holly was fading fast and her only hope was to rush her the six miles to his surgery to get her onto a drip and emergency treatment, but she didn't make it to the surgery.

Our vet conducted a post-mortem and sent off samples for analysis – which confirmed the dreaded parvovirus. Holly must have been incubating the disease when Sue rescued her. We discussed with our vet the implications of having parvovirus in the kennels. Although they were technically under the same roof, Holly had not yet mixed with any of the other dogs, except her puppies of course. However, her kennel door opened onto the same corridor as all the other kennels and Holly had been exercised in the same grass paddock used by all the other dogs.

Our vet was very concerned. He said that the pups were almost certain to die and that we should expect up to half of the other 25 dogs in the kennels to succumb to the disease. He advised us to close the kennels to any further intake for at least six months.

When the vet had left we called a staff conference. None of the dogs in the kennels were vaccinated against any disease because when Sue and I took over we decided to adhere to the anti-vivisection principles of the sanctuary's founders, the Duchess of Hamilton and Miss Lind-af-Hageby. We believed as they did, that the key to health was good nutrition and a life free from distress. We had designed the kennels to provide conditions compatible with the requirements of pack canines and although we had taken in many scores of dogs from all sorts of backgrounds, and occasionally would remove for treatment a dog which exhibited signs of disease shortly after arrival, no disease ever spread within the kennels.

We believed totally in our system of keeping dogs. Pack company, good food, dedicated and intelligent staff, keeping the kennels scrupulously dry, stimulating exercise – these were the principles we believed would keep our dogs in a state of ease – free from *dis-ease*. Holly's death from parvovirus was now to put our principles to the test.

In fact we took only one extra precaution. All our dogs had been given at least one daily garlic pill (Denes herbal products). We merely doubled the dose for all the dogs. Our vet's gloomy predictions failed to materialise and Holly's four pups thrived and grew into bouncy, healthy dogs – all of which were homed either with or through members of staff. Not one of the pups or any of the other dogs became in the slightest ill and our dog rescue and rehoming work carried on uninterrupted. We continued to rely on the belief that well-nourished and happy animals (and people) have a high immunity to most diseases.

We continued to work under this principle for our entire seven years of taking in and rehoming dogs. Although it was safe to assume that some of the stray and unwanted dogs we took into Ferne had been vaccinated against distemper, leptospirosis and other dog diseases, most were not and no dog was ever vaccinated within Ferne – no matter how long it stayed with us. Of course our vets frowned on this, but they had been educated and trained in an 'animal health industry' worth untold billions of pounds which itself kills millions of animals in experiments, testing drugs and perfecting new techniques. Vaccines, drugs and chemical wormers are dispensed by the veterinary profession by the ton in the same way as unnecessary drugs are dispensed to human patients by the medical profession. And yet, good advice, good nutrition and de-feating high levels of stress would do so much more to defeat disease than all the drugs in the world.

Vaccination of dogs is in my view one of the greatest scandals. A veterinary friend once confided in me that vaccinations represent most vets' 'bread and butter'. Vets advise clients to have their young puppies vaccinated against dog diseases such as distemper, lepto-spirosis, infectious canine hepatitis and para-influenza and then periodically send cards to the owners 'reminding' them that the dog needs boosters. There is a huge 'mark-up' on the cost of vac-cines and a dog which lives twelve years and is given regular boosters would bring a guaranteed income for the vet of hundreds of pounds irrespective of any neutering, illnesses or injuries that any dog may be expected to suffer in a long life. If the owners of all the nation's seven million dogs and eight million cats took their vet's advice and had all the recommended vaccinations and boosters, the UK's 8,500 veterinary surgeons would be rich doing nothing else but vaccinating dogs and cats.

When parvovirus first arrived in the UK in the 1970s there was a media-hyped panic. There was no vaccine and vets all over the country advised their clients to have their dogs vaccinated with an unproven cat vaccine. Dog owners queued around the block and paid outrageously inflated prices to have a feline enteritis vaccine injected into their precious animals. One leading vet told me at the time that he was ashamed of his profession over many of its members' blatant opportunism.

Most of us humans are also vaccinated as children, but we don't get a card every year asking us to go to the doctor for 'boosters'. The NHS simply could not afford it and the medical profession doesn't think it worthwhile in terms of protecting human health. So why should it be necessary for animals? My personal view is that vaccines should be reserved for animals which, because of some excessive stress or malnourishment, have reduced immunity and may need some extra protection from diseases they are likely to encounter. It is also a fact that not only can vaccines cause massive damage in some animals (and people), but that they are not always 100 per cent effective in protecting an individual from the disease.

Similarly, I think there is an over-emphasis on the worming of domestic animals. Worming chemicals can cause severe damage to delicate internal tissues, cause diarrhoea and dehydration. All animals and their parasites have evolved together for countless thousands of years and well-nourished animals can easily cope with a few parasitic worms. Giving dogs garlic, for instance, will prevent over-infestation while not completely ridding the animal of every trace of the parasite. It sounds like a good idea to remove all traces of worms with a chemical scourer, but it should be remembered that an animal with no worms at all will cease to make antibodies against them. This is fine until the animal becomes reinfected, and with no natural resistance is more severely affected. Yet more chemical wormer is needed to clear them out, until the animal picks up more worms, and so it goes on. From the veterinary chemical companies and the veterinary profession's point of view, this is fine as it means more profits, but it is largely unnecessary and sometimes dangerous medication. I knew of a goat which had lived to nine years old without ever being wormed. It went to an animal sanctuary where the sanctuary's vet insisted that the animal be wormed. It was dead a fortnight later – a post-mortem revealed severe worm infestation!

Vets recommend that all cats and dogs be regularly and frequently wormed – even if the animal is sleek and healthy and there is no sign of the presence of such parasites. In my view wormers should only be used when an animal needs some help in overcoming an over-abundance of the parasites. To me, regular and frequent worming is virtually the same as giving antibiotics to animals which are not ill – just in case they become ill. We now hear more and more about 'super-bugs' which are resistant to antibiotics because of the irresponsible way in which such drugs have been unnecessarily prescribed in the past. They have been added to the food of poultry and other factory farmed animals as growth-promoters, and to keep the animals alive in unnatural, unhygienic and stressful conditions. We need to be more careful about all medicines and drugs in the future. How many cats suffered from the trendy idea promoted by the veterinary profession to put 'flea-collars' on cats? What a daft idea, making an animal wear a permanent collar of poison next to its skin and from which toxic fumes were emanating all day and night. We came across several cat owners who complained that their pets' behaviour had changed drastically within days of the collar being fitted. Others told of skin damage and it is quite common now to see black cats with a thin white band of fur around their necks where once a lethal flea collar was fitted. I was pleased that the RSPCA launched a high profile public attack on the use of these dangerous collars, but even today these deadly collars are sold in pet shops, supermarkets and even veterinary surgeries.

Our own experience at Ferne was that modern veterinary drugs could be extremely valuable in emergencies, but that in normal circumstances the less drastic herbal and homeopathic remedies were perfectly adequate. We didn't have time to save Holly because of her appalling physical condition after eighteen months running stray in the housing estates of Bridgwater and the final drain of her pups on her physical resources. But she was the only dog we lost from disease in seven years. Hundreds more thrived and found new lives in Ferne's care.

I can remember so many of them. Goldie, an old golden retriever who lost her home because she started to go blind; Danny, a black Boxer cross who wanted to fight every other dog in the world; Patch, the Jack Russell who had had five homes and lost them all for 'aggressive behaviour' which for some reason was not once repeated at Ferne; Sacco and Vanzetti, two anarchist black labradors aged six months used as guard dogs until they escaped and worried sheep. They were in our kennels for years before they each found new homes – and settled in beautifully; Winny, dumped at the gate in the early hours of the morning with her new-born pup; Petra, rescued after being tied to a tea-chest in a farmyard for the first eighteen months of her life; the list is endless.

The main reason for this ever-growing queue of unwanted and ill-treated animals, is simply that there are not enough controls on breeding. It is simply crazy that thousands of perfectly healthy dogs and cats are destroyed every day while breeders are permitted to produce as many as they wish for profit. The breeders of pedigree dogs and cats would argue no doubt that it is the uncontrolled breeding of mongrels and 'moggies' which cause the surplus dog and cat populations, but in fact we found (and other animal homes agree) that 30 per cent of the dogs we took in were pedigree animals – and some of them extremely expensive at that. For instance we took in a red setter whose owners had paid £130 for him (at 1975 prices) and yet he spent the next three years tied up underneath the stairs. He came to us because he was 'uncontrollable' – surprise, surprise!

In Britain we could take several steps to relieve the misery caused by the over-population of dogs. Firstly a new local authority licence and national registration scheme should be introduced; with fees of around £10 annually for neutered animals and £50 for any unneutered dog or bitch. The revenue should be used to employ local dog wardens and the provide holding kennels for strays.

Breeding for sale should be strictly controlled and the breeding of certain deformed breeds prohibited. For instance, a woman once brought in a tiny Chihuahua named Barney – in her handbag! She said she couldn't keep it any longer because it messed in the house.

She pointed out a slight misalignment in one of his front legs – the result of a break sustained when he jumped off a chair. Our vet saw Barney one day and advised us in a very matter-of-fact way that we should try to keep him out of the orchard because a Chihuahua's skull is so thin that an apple dropping on him could kill him instantly. What are we doing breeding such physical freaks? As it happened, Barney was every bit as much a dog as the rest of our pack of 'yardies' – which he joined with gusto. He was perfectly clean in the house from the day he arrived; all he needed was to be treated as a dog, instead of as a toy carried around in a handbag.

There are plenty of other pedigree dogs being bred for profit and which suffer blighted lives due to inbred physical and mental deformities. Bull-dogs and Pekinese, for instance, have difficulty breathing through their strangled and flattened airways because squashed noses are demanded by the breed standard. Consequently these unfortunate dogs spend their lives licking off the mucus which continually runs down their noses as nature attempts to wash-out the 'obstruction' And neither breed could run fifty yards without being in danger of collapsing. There is no excuse for inflicting such a life on a dog and neither is there any justification for mutilating a dog's tail to suit a catalogue.

Cats

The cats of Ferne lived in the luxury of a small wooden bungalow and when we first took over they also had free access to the sanctuary's 36 acres. However, this degree of freedom took a considerable toll on the local wildlife and after finding a goldcrest, Britain's smallest bird, dead on the cattery floor, we decided that we should restrict the freedom of the cats by fencing the garden that surrounded the cattery bungalow. Britain's massive domestic cat population of up to nine million only have to kill an average of one small animal or bird a month each for the total to reach 100 million wasted deaths.

It is a miracle that any small birds survive, given the size of the cat population and the widespread use of highly toxic chemicals and slug pellets by farmers and gardeners. It always amazes me that so many people are quick to write to their local newspaper complaining that magpies or sparrow hawks kill and eat some small birds, and yet choose to ignore the fact that their gardens are awash with poisons and constantly patrolled by deadly feline predators.

One cat who didn't represent much of a threat to Ferne's wildlife and who therefore retained his freedom to roam the sanctuary, was Cassidy. He had lost half of a front leg in a 'gin' trap, that evil instrument of torture so beloved by gamekeepers up to and (for some) even beyond its legal abolition in 1958.

As a child, my first experience of man's brutality to wild animals was finding a live rabbit held by the shredded remains of one of its hind legs in such a 'gin' trap. (The word 'gin' is derived from 'engine' – the trap's spring mechanism which slams serrated metal jaws shut when an animal treads on a metal plate). Even today it is not uncommon for some criminal gamekeepers to set such traps on the top of posts to trap and smash the legs of birds of prey such as owls or buzzards. I dread to contemplate how many scores of millions of animals, both wild and domestic have been maimed or killed in 'gin' traps over the centuries in Britain alone.

Cassidy was a cheerful old tabby-cat despite bronchial catarrh and gradually failing kidneys. We put him on herbal kidney pills and garlic tablets which improved his health and kept him well enough to permanently stake a claim to a storage heater and to greet every human visitor to the sanctuary with a prod of his stump!

Another old character already a long-term resident when we arrived at Ferne, was Tabatha, 'Queen of the cattery'. Her record card revealed that she was at least fifteen years old and had been a stray cat in Australia before being adopted and later emigrating to the United Kingdom with her family. Some domestic crisis had led to the family breaking up and Tabatha had been taken in by Ferne. Now she was cantankerous, elderly and deaf, but very much top-cat in the cattery. Woe betide any moggy which took a fancy to Tabatha's basket! If she returned to find an interloper, she would box their ears and drive them out without making a sound. No cat ever stood up to her.

As the years passed, Tabatha gradually weakened and spent more time asleep until one day she would not leave her basket for food. As she didn't seem to be in any discomfort we left her alone except for offering her water every hour or so during the day. The next day I brought her into my office so that I could keep her under observation while I caught up on a backlog of paperwork. Later in the day she seemed to drift into unconsciousness and a short period of laboured breathing eventually ended with a single, long sigh. I watched closely for a few moments and then ran my hand along her still body. Feeling no signs of life, I left the office to quickly tour the sanctuary to tell the staff, 'The Queen is dead!'

However, within minutes I had to repeat the tour to inform everyone that when I had returned to the office, Tabatha was breathing steadily again, but still quite unconscious! Twice more she stopped breathing and started again before her tough old spirit went wherever animal spirits go.

Anyone who works for any period of time in an animal home learns a lot about death. With more than two hundred animals of many species, often with a history of abandonment or cruelty, and in a sanctuary with a policy of reserving destruction only for the relief of incurable suffering, one is sure to see many animals die. Euthanasia is the one area of existence where animals are treated better than human beings, but particularly in cases of old age, not all deaths involve pain. It doesn't really matter how long it takes to die, as long as there is no pain. There is no point in paying a veterinary surgeon to waste his skills and his drugs in hastening the death of an animal that is perfectly capable of dying at its own natural pace.

I think I felt sorrier for cats which had lost their homes than for any other homeless animal. In my experience virtually all dogs quickly forget their owners provided they are quickly thrust into a new 'pack' – canine or human. Cats suffer far more stress from such upheavals and at such times the distress can be so great that the cat will be vulnerable to disease and may refuse to eat for days.

Tissy was a tortoiseshell cat of thirteen years, much worshipped by her elderly owner. The couple were parted due to the old lady being forced by increasing frailty to move into residential accommodation where the rule was 'No Pets'. Tissy's heartbroken owner tearfully left her in our care. What sort of society is this which subjects a frail and lonely old lady to such heartbreak? It's bad enough treating animals like unfeeling objects without causing such misery to our own species!

Tissy would not eat for a week. Eventually we had to take it in turns to give her constant human companionship until at last she began to purr when stroked and would then take an interest in food. If you walked away she would promptly stop eating until the procedure was repeated. A month later she had put her weight back on, appeared much brighter and we began to think that she might even be lucky enough to find a new home. But then she started refusing food again – this time due to bad teeth and infected gums. Our vet removed the lot after which she gradually recovered and slowly adapted successfully to her new life in the cattery. I often wondered if the old lady adapted too.

Some of the cats we took in were 'rescued' strays. One of the most memorable was Wildy, a jet-black spitting, hissing bundle of savagery. She had been living wild in the hedgerows of Somerset and regularly producing kittens. Local cat lovers had managed to catch the kittens when young and find homes for them, but Wildy always managed to escape capture. One day, she was seen entering a shed and a brave lady dashed forward and slammed the door shut. But how to get her out? A local gamekeeper was called (he would not have been my choice!) and he agreed to try to get her into a cage. He ventured into the shed fully armoured in gauntlets, goggles and helmet; and after a furious fight emerged bloody but victorious, with Wildy caged.

We decided to put Wildy into a room in the house so that we could sit in with her during the evenings to get her used to being in close proximity to human beings. We carried Wildy into the room, shut the door and opened the cage. But we had made a huge mistake. We had not blocked off the fireplace and in a flash Wildy was up the chimney and soot was crashing down into the fireplace.

There was no way of extricating her from the ledge she had

The cattery garden

found ten feet up inside the chimney. All we could do was to put down bowls of food and water and leave the room. The next morning the food was gone, but she had returned to her sooty hiding place. After a couple of days she abandoned the chimney and had opted instead for a hiding place we had created in the corner of the room, Gradually she would eat with one of us in the room watching, although we were a bit worried about her watery eyes which we surmised was a result of the soot and dust in the chimney.

But there was nothing we could do about it as she was still far too ferocious to handle. Then suddenly she went down with cat flu and became so weak and ill that we were sure she would die. In the hospital unit she was too weak to resist the veterinary treatment and constant nursing during which we fed her liquid with a dropper. As her strength began to return she also began to respond to human touch and by the time she moved into the main cattery she had become the most affectionate and clinging cat in the sanctuary!

Wobbly was a very attractive fluffy grey and white kitten, one of a litter found on a local rubbish dump. He had been spotted falling about drunkenly and shaking his head violently and upon examination our vet diagnosed meningitis and advised destruction. As a last resort we rang a spiritual healer friend in Cornwall who agreed to put Wobbly on her 'absent healing' list. The very next day Wobbly was running around the garden playing with the other kittens – the only symptom remaining being a slightly wobbly gait which remained with him for the rest of his long life.

Finding homes for adult cats is a nightmare, as anyone connected with animal rescue will confirm. Any adult cat with less than perfect looks had no chance whatsoever of finding a new home. Charlie White was seventeen and had been in the sanctuary for most of his life. His problem was solar dermatitis on his ears – a condition in which the sun causes the albino-like skin to continually blister and scab. The irritation causes the cat to scratch the ears sore and eventually they can end up in a real mess. In the summer months we tried all sorts of ointments and creams but nothing seemed to screen out the damaging sunlight. Eventually our vet had to surgically remove one ear completely and trim the damaged edges from the other. Then we had a brainwave. Boot polish! What better way of preventing the sun's rays from getting through to the sensitive skin? After checking the ingredients, our vet confirmed that this would cause no harm and all-white Charlie finished up with black ears – well, one black ear and one black patch around what was once his other ear.

This worked a treat, and for the first time for years Charlie was free of irritation and could lie out in the sun without suffering damage. He was very old and his meow had long ago been replaced by a silent gasp, but he remained first in the queue for his food, dribbled with pleasure when picked up and cuddled, and was friendly with every living thing.

As I write this account of my years employed as manager of Ferne, the names and images of cat after cat after cat come into my mind. Our involvement with them was often born out of someone else's brutality or callousness. But, equally often the arrival at Ferne of an unhappy homeless animal was associated with some human tragedy – death, divorce, redundancy or homelessness. In a few cases a pet was given up in a family's decision to emigrate to a completely new life, and this is the reason for the arrival of the very first cat we took into the new sanctuary, and the strangest animal story in my life – the story of Loki.

When we arrived at Ferne there were already sixteen cats in residence. We decided that we would not take in any more until we had wired-in the cattery garden and put an end to the cats' freedom to slaughter the local wildlife. However, we made an exception for Loki, a slim, sleek, spayed female, all black with a white tip to her long thin tail. The family were emigrating to Australia and could not take the cat. When we visited the family they explained that Loki sometimes exhibited a nasty temper, had never been affectionate and preferred her own company. After we had written down her details and accepted a substantial donation to Ferne, Loki was handed over to my wife and immediately settled affectionately around her neck. In fact she was so relaxed that we didn't even bother putting her into a travelling cage and during the short car journey back to Ferne, Loki sat happily on Sue's shoulder. A few days later I wrote in my work diary; 'Loki is a real character. She has settled in very well and really enjoys cattery life. She skips along the walls and banks, and turns up all over the place – a very happy and adventurous cat.'

When we enclosed the cattery garden, none of the cats seemed to mind the restriction, except Loki. She became nervous of the other cats. If they came close she would freeze as if petrified, but she never hissed, spat or fought with them. She ate well and always looked in gleaming good health, but became venomous if picked up – a trait which we felt would ensure she would never find a new home.

More than a year later a local family visited us in the hope of finding a new cat. We took them into the cattery, where they instantly fell for Loki. I warned them she sometimes displayed a nasty streak and that the children might prefer choosing one of the gentler cats which would really appreciate affection and a home life. But they wouldn't consider any cat but Loki. I even mentioned that the word Loki was an old Norse word used to call up the devil, but the man laughingly said that her name made her even more attractive!

I asked them to consider it for a week and then ring us if they still wanted Loki. Sure enough, we received the call, and the next day we delivered Loki to her new home. The parents and two daughters aged ten and fourteen all knelt on the floor while I opened the travelling cage. Loki stalked out and, appearing quite unconcerned, toured the room peering and sniffing in each corner before jumping up onto the settee, settling down and purring loudly. A bowl of food appeared, but I said that she might not eat for a day or so until she felt settled. To my amazement Loki jumped off the settee, tucked into the food and then went to each member of her new family purring and fluffing herself against their legs.

The family really impressed me. The mother was the sort of cool, confident and intelligent woman one imagined could cope in any crisis. The husband was outgoing and friendly and the children well-mannered and polite. The elder daughter had an ambition to be a veterinary surgeon and we invited her to visit Ferne whenever she wanted to accompany Sue on her veterinary rounds.

We had seen enough, and after advising the family to keep Loki in for a week or two until the was thoroughly familiar with her surroundings, we left. A few days later Loki's new mistress phoned to say that their new cat was already going out and about, always came when called and loved being fussed. She said she had seen no sign of the Loki's 'evil streak' we had warned them about. I told her I was delighted that Loki had settled so well and that perhaps it had merely been her restriction in the cattery which had caused her anti-social behaviour at Ferne.

Three weeks later I was in Chard picking up some supplies and I bought the local newspaper. The front page story was of a tragedy in which a local woman had drunk a cupful of Paraquat weed-killer and had died in hospital. Apparently she drunk the poison and then phoned relatives and told them what she had done. An ambulance had been sent to her house, but nothing could be done to save her. As I sat in the car glancing through the story, my blood almost froze when I saw the name of the dead woman. It was Loki's new mistress!

For several minutes I was shaking too much to start the car and drive back to Ferne. I discussed the situation with Sue. Should we ring her husband and offer to take Loki back while he came to terms with the tragedy? Or would it be better for the bereaved family to have Loki to care for? In the end we decided to do nothing. How do you raise the issue of a cat with a family which has suffered such trauma?

On making notes on Loki's card later that day, my heart thumped a little louder when noticed that Loki had come to Ferne on February 29th and that the date we had delivered her to her new home was Friday, 13th. Feeling even more uncomfortable, I noted that she was the thirteenth cat re-homed that year. One's mind can start to run amok once it starts down that route! I remembered visiting the home and thinking that the lady was the type who could cope with anything. Then I remembered that 'Loki' was an ancient name for the devil. My mind raced back to the day she had telephoned me and in our conversation had said that Loki always came when called. I imagined her at her back door calling 'Loki, Loki' into the darkness.

It was several weeks before I plucked up courage to ring the family. The man answered the phone and greeted me with his friendly voice when I told him who I was. He told me Loki was fine and very well. Neither he nor I mentioned his wife.

Goats

Goats are my favourite animals. I think it is their confidence and slightly arrogant nature. We quickly built up a herd of a dozen unwanted goats at the sanctuary, which not only had a two acre fenced paddock to roam in, but were also out most of the days browsing the hedgerows and grazing the fields. A member of staff would treck out across the fields to check them every hour or two, and late in the afternoon a call would bring them skipping, dancing and mock-fighting down the hills to the yard for a troughful of bran, maize and goat-nuts. They would then queue up to clamber up a ramp and through a cave-like hole we had knocked in the wall of our big barn, and settle down in deep straw to chew the cud.

The only problem with goats is that they can devastate any form of vegetation and have no idea what plants are toxic to them until too late. In the wild the matriarchal nanny-goat teaches young members of the herd what plants to avoid, by attacking, butting and stamping on the offending flora. The knowledge had been passed onto her the same way. Domestic goats don't have the advantage of such an education and consequently if they break their tether they will rush to the nearest tree or bush and gorge themselves on it no matter whether it is lethal such as yew, or dangerous, such as laurel. Unless you have spent a night nursing a goat which has eaten too much laurel, I can assure you, reader, that you don't really know the meaning of the term 'projectile vomiting'.

However, our experience is that free-range goats rarely poison themselves to that extent. They tend to take a mouthful or two of one plant, then move to another, and so on and so on. The effect seems to be to that no one plant is taken in enough bulk to create a problem, or perhaps the ingredients of one plant counteract those of another. Our goats even stripped yew bark and leaves without harm because they were also eating many other plants around.

The saddest thing about goats is that they are often tethered on a long chain, all alone, and with no shelter. Goats love company and absolutely hate the rain. In a way it's a shame that goats are so tolerant and have such nice natures – otherwise they might not be treated so badly.

Sam was a black Nubian goat rescued from a middle-class family which had abandoned conventional suburban life in favour of a self-sufficient 'back to nature' life in a caravan. Why they obtained a neutered male goat is a mystery, but presumably it fitted in with the 'hippie' image. Unfortunately he had been tethered in one spot so long, and was so malnourished, that he was suffering from rickets, which in addition to badly overgrown hooves, left him painfully crippled. Nubian goats with their long droopy ears look sad enough as it is without being so cruelly neglected.

Within a couple of months at Ferne, free-ranging with the herd and being able to feed on a wide variety of vegetation and supplementary cereals, he soon returned to full fitness, his sleek black hair glistening in the sun.

Another favourite was Belle, once a champion Toggenburg goat who was reputed to have produced two gallons of milk per day. How many kids she gave birth to and was robbed of so that humans could steal their milk, we never knew, but the exploitation was sufficient high to result in such severe mastitis that a veterinary surgeon pronounced her incurable. Hence she came to Ferne with one udder as heavy and solid as a house-brick, and so swollen and full that her teats were almost touching the ground.

Sue immediately milked out the good udder and in doing so made a life-long friend of Belle. Then she set to work on the solid udder which was so infected that abscesses kept breaking out. Twice every day, Sue called Belle into the house and for an hour at a time would massage the solid udder in an attempt to break down the mass of solidified milk. Before starting each session, using a syringe without a needle, Sue would inject her own brew of dock leaves and garlic up through the teat into the milk channel. This continued day after day with very little progress, with fresh abscesses breaking out every couple of days. Then slowly the solid lump began to soften and break up, diminishing gradually as Sue squeezed out the disintegrating 'cheese', until after a full nine months of this daily routine Belle's udders were pink and healthy, and her milk smooth and pure. Throughout all those hours of discomfort while Sue kneaded the swollen udder and squeezed pus from many abscesses, not once did Belle complain or refuse to come when called in for the treatment.

Belle went on to live to old age in the sanctuary with her milk being given to the pigs or dogs for a treat, or for the benefit of sick kittens in the surgery.

One of the holiday attractions for visitors to the North coast of Devon is the Valley of Rocks at Lynmouth. This spectacular gorge was also the home of an assorted herd of 'wild' goats which wandered free and which a casual tourist might think enjoyed a wonderful free life in perfect goat terrain. We were told that the local Council regarded the goats as an extra draw to the public and employed a 'part-time' goatherd to keep and eye on their welfare.

Indeed, these days it is claimed that the herd is made up of the old breed on Northumberland wild goats, but when we visited in the 1970s they were a mixture of abandoned and unwanted domestic goats dumped in the valley by their owners. The valley offered them a free-ranging life, but a sparse food supply and in the winter harsh, biting winds and driving rain which would be a challenge even to truly wild goats.

Sue and I visited the valley one day and managed to get close enough to the herd to see that several of them were lame and suffering from overgrown hooves; others had cuts and small wounds and one white Saanen was obviously in great pain from severely swollen udders. She had clearly given birth recently but there was no sign of a young kid with the herd. Her udders, which unusually had four teats rather than two, were banging painfully against her back legs and were grazed and bleeding from being dragged over the rocks and through the gorse and thorns.

We spent a couple of hours stalking the herd and after a short chase managed to grab 'Rocky'– as we later named her. We started to milk her out, but with one udder half empty, she suddenly broke free and scrambled up the rocks to join the huge horned Billy-goat calling for her. He then led the herd high up onto a cliff overlooking the sea, where we dared not follow.

We went back into the town and made a few enquires – finishing up in the Town Clerk's office where we protested about the condition of the goats. He seemed most concerned and told us that a local man was employed by the Council as a part-time goatherd to monitor the goats' welfare. He assured us that he would take action immediately to resolve the issue.

A week later, we returned and found that nothing had been done and that Rocky was still suffering. We found the local Mayor, told him of previous visit and that we were considering launching a private prosecution against the Council for cruelty. The Mayor immediately spoke to the Town Clerk and afterwards told us that the Clerk had been in the course of organising the construction of a permanent paddock in the gorge in which the goats could be captured for periodic examination, foot-trimming and treatment. We told the Mayor that we approved of the idea, but that if Rocky was not treated quickly she would suffer mastitis. He invited us to try and catch her and take her back to Ferne. A phone call to the Hunt Saboteurs Association soon brought half a dozen young volunteers to Lynmouth to help us catch a few of the goats so that we could trim their feet and to hold Rocky while Sue milked out several pints of milk from her swollen udders.

Soon she was on her way back to Ferne with us to start a new, somewhat easier life with a very different herd of goats.

The two leaders of our goat-herd were Moss and Dock, two neutered billies we had brought with us when we arrived at Ferne. We had taken them in as ill, unwanted kids when we were living in the village of Berwick St John near Shaftesbury where they grew into strong and sturdy animals. Before we arranged for them to be neutered, we discovered that when we were out one day, a local man had walked his in-season nanny goat to our home and without our permission had mated her with both Moss and Dock.

We were outraged as we knew that the man kept goats to produce kids which, if they were male he would kill and eat, and if female keep to become new breeding and milk-producing machines. The man was clearly embarrassed that he had been found out, as mating

Dock, second in command of the herd

animals with a neighbour's without permission is a major sin in any rural community.

We came to a negotiated settlement, that when his nanny gave birth, he would keep any female, but would hand over any male offspring to us after weaning. Before the kids were born we had moved to Somerset to take over the management of the new Ferne

Annimal Sanctuary, but we kept a careful eye on the calendar and when we calculated that the nanny goat should have given birth, Sue rang the owner. He excitedly told her that his goat had given birth to triplets – two males and a female. Sue arranged to call him again in a month to arrange a convenient time to collect the two Billies, but when the time came, Sue rang, only to be told that he had already killed and eaten one of the male kids. We were outraged and Sue told him in no uncertain terms what we thought of his treachery, but he couldn't care less and slammed the phone down on her – not a wise thing to do with Sue!

The next day Sue drove to Berwick St John to 'have it out' with the family. No-one was in, but the nanny goat was tethered in the lane and her two kids grazing free nearby. Sue popped a note in their letter-box to say she had collected the two kids, which were soon speeding back to Ferne on the back seat of our car.

That evening, the phone rang and a very angry voice was complaining bitterly that we had stolen his goats, deprived his children of meat, stopped his family becoming rich from breeding goats, and had generally destroyed the world as he knew it. We told him that he should have kept his side of the bargain we had struck after his clandestine use of our billies' sexual prowess. 'I am coming now to collect my goats,' he yelled down the phone before ringing off.

This was pretty worrying. He was a six foot five inches tall Dutchman and big with it. He had no transport, but I knew that he would already have set off, hitch-hiking the fifty miles from Berwick St John in Wiltshire to Wambrook on the Somerset-Devon border. I rang the local police and explained the situation and they told me to call them again the moment he arrived. Within two hours he was striding down our drive and as soon as we spotted him, we rang the police. By the time our 'guest' was sitting in our kitchen drinking coffee, a police car was pulling into our yardand we were joined by two police officers. They were both known well to us as we had a contract to care for stray dogs brought into Chard police station.

The sergeant took over proceedings and asked the Dutchman to make his case. He did so, repeating time and time again that we had stolen his two goats, that we could keep the billy kid, but that he wanted the nanny. We went through our story – right back to him mating his old nanny with our then unneutered billies, without our permission. The sergeant was brilliant – clearly relishing the role of judge. The conversation went something like this.

'Let's get this straight. Did you have permission to mate your nanny with Mr Bryant's goats?'

'No.'

'Why didn't you ask?'

'Because I knew he would say no.'

'Did you offer payment to Mr Bryant for the service?'

'No.'

'But you came to an agreement about the offspring?'

'Yes.'

'And what was that agreement?'

'I would keep any nanny kids and Mr and Mrs Bryant would have any billies.'

'And what young did your nanny have?'

'Two billies and a nanny.'

'That's three kids.'

'Yes.'

'And you agreed that Mr and Mrs Bryant could have two.'

'Yes.'

'Well, they've got their two.'

'No, no, I was to keep the nanny.'

'So where's the other one you promised them?'

'I killed it – to feed my family.'

'Well, well! So, not only do you admit to unlawfully breeding your goat with theirs, and that you didn't even offer payment for the service, but you also admit you've killed and eaten their goat!'

The Dutchman sat deflated and huddled over the table staring into his empty cup. I felt sorry for him. 'I'm not leaving here without my nanny,' he mumbled.

'Oh, but you are, I'm afraid,' said the Sergeant firmly. 'I suggest you go home and consult a solicitor. It's past midnight and these good folks want to get to sleep. We can give you a lift and put you on the road home,' offered the policeman.

'I'm not leaving without my goat,' said the Dutchman, defiantly straightening up, folding his arms and glaring challengingly first at the Sergeant and then at the constable.

The latter took my arm and pulled me gently into the hall. 'We cannot legally ask him to leave your property,' he said quietly. 'You have to ask him to leave and put your hand on his arm while you do so. If he refuses or resists we will arrest him.'

Nervously, I did as suggested and to my relief the huge Dutchman rose and buttoned his coat.

'Do you want a lift, son?' asked the Sergeant kindly.

'No, I'll walk,' he replied, striding into the hall to the back door.

'Warn him you are leaving a guard dog free,' whispered the constable, realising, as I did, that the Dutchman had no intention of giving up so easily.

I shouted the warning to the grey shape rapidly disappearing up the drive, but there was no reply.

'He's not going anywhere,' I told the two policemen. 'He'll hang around until you've gone and then come back for his kid.'

'Where are the goats?' asked the constable, grinning when I said they were fast asleep in our lounge!

'We can't stay any longer,' said the sergeant. 'If he does come back give us a call and we'll pick him up and stick him in the cells for a few hours.'

After thanking the two officers for their patient help, I trotted across to the kennels and let Duke our large Alsatian into the exercise paddock. Anyone sneaking the long way round to the barns would have to pass the dog paddock and even if Duke's ferocious bark didn't frighten them off then at least we would be warned of their approach.

Back in the house we put all the lights on and I patrolled the outside veranda pathetically wielding a large rusty sword we had found earlier in an outbuilding. Sure enough, an hour later, Duke's deep-throated roar suddenly erupted and the chain-link fence rattled as the dog threw himself at it. Then I heard the Dutchman's footsteps sprinting up the drive to the road; he was not to know Duke was safely confined, and clearly decided not to take a chance on my warning being a bluff.

We heard nothing more for a couple of weeks and then discovered that the Dutchman had written complaining to the sanctuary's board of Trustees that we had 'stolen' his goats, thus depriving his family of fresh meat and the basis of a future milking herd. Unfortunately for him all the sanctuary Trustees were vegetarians; he might as well have admitted being a badger-baiter! All the Dutchman got for his trouble was a venomous letter from Lady

Tansy and Sedge

Dowding with a small cheque for (as Lady Dowding put it) his 'pound of flesh'. We named the two kids Sedge and Tansy and they were soon skipping along the sanctuary's dry-stone walls and facing a lifetime of freedom from exploitation.

One of the most vivacious of the goats was a young Pigmy female named Bracken. To her life was a total joy. She had mock battles with every living creature which crossed her path – prancing to and fro, head tilted at a threatening angle, trying to tempt a baffled duck or a bewildered chicken into a fight. We soon learned not to allow any car to be parked in the yard as Bracken would delight in springing onto the bonnet and thence onto the roof where she would dance as 'king of the castle' causing dents and scratches to the paint work.

One day while we were eating breakfast in the kitchen, she suddenly sprang onto the kitchen window sill. Peering at us sitting at the table she came straight through the window, showering us in glass and landing on the table with surprise written all over her face, but without a trace of panic.

Goats are famous for not panicking in situations when lesser creatures would be crashing around in terror. I've been told that at one time race-horse owners commonly kept a goat in the stables, so that if fire broke out, there would be a good chance of the goat quietly leading out the much flightier equines. I don't know whether the story is myth or not, but goats faced with danger certainly seem much calmer than animals such as sheep. For instance, sheep which

Bracken — lovable vandal

sight a dog will rapidly move and join up in a large group. If the flock is attacked they will scatter in total disarray. Goats will run to find a way to get their backs to a wall or tree and then face the dog head down to deter the attacker with its horns.

However, there is something deep in the nature of goats which may be responsible for their mythological place in sorcery and the occult. The horns may associate them with 'the devil', and as Bracken demonstrated, there is plenty of devilment in goats! But there may be something else. One day, my brother Bill brought a party of mentally-handicapped children to the sanctuary from

Yeovil. Most of the children were sufferers from Down's syndrome who enjoyed making contact with the animals as much as the animals enjoyed the experience. However, one lad, a tall twelve year-old, was held tightly by the hand by my brother. The boy had an ungainly gait; his head tilted to one side and his eyes constantly peering upwards. He appeared to be completely unaware of or disinterested in what was happening around him, and yet as a chicken crossed his path he lashed out at it with his foot and would have pressed the attack had not Bill kept him in a firm grip. The strange thing was that he seemed to aware of what was beneath his feet despite his eyes being fixed on the sky.

My brother led the lad over to the goats' paddock and stood at the large metal gate that was clad with chain-link fencing. We had decided that we wouldn't let the children into the paddock as by then we had fifteen goats and we feared they might become pretty boisterous amongst a crowd of excited children. The goats were anyway around 100 yards away grazing and ignoring the line of children gathering at the gate. I saw Dock, a big white neutered billy-goat and deputy herd leader, look up from his grazing and, all alone, begin striding towards us. By then the children had begun drifting away to see the cats and rabbits, but my brother and I remained chatting – the boy between us, his hand still in the grip of my brother, his eyes still glued to the sky. Dock kept marching towards us, the rest of the herd continuing with their feeding at the far end of the paddock. It then occurred to me that there was something strange and purposeful about Dock's approach. Our conversation stopped as Dock came straight towards the gate, his eyes firmly fixed on the boy, and without hesitation crashed his huge horns into the chain-link fencing between him and the boy. At the same instant, his eyes still on the sky, the boy loudly snarled at Dock and lashed at the gate with his foot. It was a really weird display of mutual hatred. Dock appeared to have made a bee-line for a complete stranger from a hundred yards away with the intention of attacking him. This is completely unlike normal goat behaviour and as we hurriedly moved away to join the rest of the children, Dock remained at the gate – staring intently after us.

The only other time Dock embarrassed me was one Sunday afternoon when I was showing around a group of visitors. It was a nice sunny day and all but one of the dozen or so visitors were adults. So I took them into the goats' paddock and began to explain to them each goat's history. The goats' shelter was a large stone barn with access by way of a ramp up to a platform and through a hole knocked through the wall at a height of about five feet. The idea was to make it as near as 'cave' as possible.

As the visitors were stroking the goats and listening to my 'lecture', the one child, a truculent ten-year-old boy, kept trying to climb up the ramp, at the top of which stood Dock guarding the entrance. Twice I asked the lad to come down as I could see Dock viewing him suspiciously. Twice the boy's father repeated the instruction and I could see that lad's behaviour was beginning to irritate the rest of the party. Then, as I was pointing to the location of our dog kennels to the south of the goats' paddock, there was a loud scream behind us. I spun round to see Dock standing on the platform at the top of the ramp, with the screaming boy dangling by his T shirt from one of Dock's huge horns. As I leapt forward Dock swung the boy once around his head and threw him off into the air to fall in a crumpled heap at the bottom of the ramp.

As we went to his aid, I visualised headlines of 'Child maimed at animal sanctuary', pending law-suits, council safety officers, court cases, massive damages, and me packing my suit-case. Fortunately, the whimpering boy was uninjured except for a graze on his back where Dock had thrust his horn up inside the boy's T shirt. And he got no sympathy from his father, who roughly hauled him to his feet and dusted him down saying, 'It's your own fault. You were told twice.' I caught one or two of the other visitors smirking at each other and I breathed an inward sigh of relief.

Cows and Sheep – and the Men from the Ministry!

The first sheep to arrive were lambs, Larry and Lucy (both in fact female) having been raised as orphans by a butcher! When the time came for Larry and Lucy to be slaughtered for human food the butcher could not go through with it and so they came to Ferne. One wonders what proportion of the population would be vegetarians if people had to rear and kill their own food animals? Pretty high, I would think. Perhaps it is worth mentioning here that during our management of Ferne we only recruited staff who were vegetarians or vegans, as it didn't seem logical for people to spend their working days caring for animals and their free time eating them.

Sue with Larry and Lucy

65

Larry and Lucy joined the herd of goats and soon began to adopt the attitudes and behaviour of the goats. This adaptation even began to extend to fighting techniques. When goats are sparring they often rear up on their hind legs and then fall towards each other, bringing their heads together in a resounding although apparently painless crack. Sheep, of course, fight in a different way – by using their lower centre of gravity in a rapid series of charges. It was fascinating to watch both tactics in use during mock battles between sheep and goats, and eventually we found that the sheep began to learn the goats' style and *vice versa*. When calves joined the group later, and brought yet another style of battle into the play, things really began to get complicated.

We were eventually home to a dozen goats, five sheep, three cows and a steer (castrated bull) and three pigs. The most interesting aspect of giving permanent sanctuary to animals which are normally only reared to provide milk and meat, is the attitude of the Ministry of Agriculture, Fisheries and Food.

We had a visit one day from a man who introduced himself as a Diseases of Animals Inspector of MAFF. He told us that he had been 'informed' that we had sheep at the sanctuary and that he had come to ensure that we knew that the law dictated that all sheep should be 'dipped' to combat sheep scab – a skin disease caused by mites. We showed him the sheep, explained that they were virtually pet sheep, very tame, handled every day and would never go to market or enter the human food chain. The concept of keeping sheep without the intention of either sending them to market, or breeding from them, or killing them for food was beyond the imagination of the inspector – a former police officer. I pointed out that unlike millions of other sheep, ours would not be thrown out on some hill and left to get on with it until rounded up for shearing or slaughter. I told him that any sign of trouble with parasites would be immediately noticed by the staff and would be treated immediately, so there could be no chance of them passing parasites to other sheep.

'The National Sheep Order demands that all sheep must be dipped,' insisted the inspector, before leaving us some paperwork on the specifications of the dipping solution and telling us to ring him when we intended to dip the sheep so that he could observe.

He warned me that I would be prosecuted if I failed to comply with the Order.

I did a bit of reading up on sheep scab and went to the local agriculture supplies store and read the label on the Benzine Hexachloride (BHC) sheep-dip in which we were required to dump our sheep twice within a fortnight in November. I read that the mite was wingless and could therefore be only passed from sheep to sheep. The BHC dip we were ordered to use was highly dangerous and could cause twitching, muscular incoordination, anxiety and convulsions. Operators were advised to wear complete body-covering protective clothing and not to allow the solution into waterways as it is extremely poisonous to fish. I wrote to MAFF asking for an exemption from the dipping Order on the grounds that we saw no possibility of our sheep ever catching or spreading the scab parasite, that I was not prepared to expose either the sheep or our staff to such a dangerous chemical, and that anyway we had no dipping bath or any facilities for disposing of the lethal liquid afterwards.

As a compromise I offered to dip the sheep in a herbal mixture recommended by famous farm animal herbalist Juliette de Bairaccli Levy whose book was Sue's herbal remedy bible. MAFF held a regional conference to discuss this, but refused to agree to our suggestion. Instead they sent one of their veterinary surgeons to visit us, and after examining the sheep and looking around the sanctuary, she advised me to apply for a licence under the Medicines Act to make up our own sheep dip mixture of carbolic acid and soft soap mixed proportionately and diluted in water.

So I dutifully sent off my £10 and soon I was in possession of a Medicines Act licence that gave us an alternative formula of sulphur, lime and water to the carbolic acid and soft soap mixture. Two chemists we approached told us that could not understand the MAFF definition of carbolic acid. They both said that this was in fact phenol – a highly dangerous liquid. After spending days making telephone calls to the Ministry departments and local authority County Analysts in an effort to obtain a trade name, a supplier, details of dilution and a written guarantee that the substance would not harm either the sheep or ourselves, I gave up and opted for the alternative sulphur and lime mixture. The lime was easy to obtain, but we had to order the sulphur from a Bristol company. By the time it arrived we had gone over the deadline for the dipping period and MAFF told us we would have to apply to the local council for authority to carry out a 'late' dip.

We purchased an old boiler from a local auction for heating up our mixture. and called the Diseases of Animals Inspector to arrange the day. On the morning of the 'dip' we dragged an old bath out of the field where it had been used in the past as a drinking trough, washed it out and began to fill it with the dip mixture diluted in warm water. It smelled absolutely disgusting – like a bath-full of sweaty socks! The Inspector was highly amused that we intended to dip the sheep in warm water – illustrating again the callousness with which sheep are normally treated in farming. The dipping period was November, and anyone who has seen sheep thrown into freezing sheep dip, forced to tread water for one minute and then have their heads plunged under the water with a pitchfork, should not wonder that many sheep die later of shock or exposure – let alone the effects of the toxic chemicals.

Ours were lifted bodily one at a time by five members of staff, and lowered gently into the warm bath on their backs. They appeared to quite enjoy the experience, and we just about to lift out the first one, when the Inspector shouted; 'OK, that's one minute. Now push her head under.' I queried this with the Inspector and he responded by saying that the mites flew onto the sheep's eyelids from gateposts and that therefore their heads had to be washed in the liquid. I scoffed at this and pointed out that sheep scab mites are wingless and that he was talking rubbish. 'The law is that the heads must be submerged,' he said, as he stepped forward to push Lucy's head under the foul liquid. But before he could do so, Sue, at the other end of the bath, brought her arm down with a smack, shooting a huge handful of the liquid into his face. While he staggered backwards, spluttering and spitting as he groped for a handkerchief to wipe the foul water from his face, we lifted Lucy out, and set her on her feet. She shook herself violently and then dripped quietly while she munched a few goat-nuts from a bucket.

Amazingly, the inspector said nothing, but just glowered at us. Trying to avoid his glare, we grabbed Larry and lifted her into the bath. This time the Inspector stood back several yards staring intently at his watch. 'OK,' he said after the minute's soak, but this time did not make any mention of submerging the sheep's head. Soon Larry was also contentedly munching while the yellow liquid dripped from her wool onto the yard.

The Inspector stripped off his black waterproofs and rubber boots, and stowed them in the boot of his car. As he climbed into his seat and closed his door, I approached him wondering whether I should apologise for Sue's method of defending Lucy. He was thumbing through his diary. 'Right, second dip in ten days?' he said, not looking at me as I stood at his open window. 'Same time?' I asked meekly. 'Yep,' he snapped as he started his engine, and with his electric window closing, he sped up the drive.

I really expected some official sanction against us for the humiliation he suffered at our hands. But no, he came back in ten days, stood well away from us with his stop watch, while we went through the dipping procedure again with Larry and Lucy.

It was not long before we had five sheep and the dipping exercise became a real chore. But during our whole period at Ferne, our sheep never went through the terrifying plunge into the freezing, lethal liquid experienced by millions of sheep every year. Twenty years later the media was reporting that farmers and their wives were complaining that they were suffering severe ill-health from using sheep dips containing BHC (now banned in the UK) and the organo-phosphates which came later and which are at least, if not more, as lethal. I saw them interviewed on television farming programmes and found myself shouting at the screen shouting things like, 'Why didn't you read the label on the tin?' and 'You were quite happy to throw your sheep in it, weren't you?' But, I suppose, they deserve some sympathy. When the 'men from the Ministry' arrive, they can be very intimidating to someone whose living depends on sticking to the rules. The inspector we dealt with was clearly used to farmers grovelling in his presence, and that may be why he seemed completely flummoxed when Sue scooped a huge slurp of foul, yellowish sheep-dip into his face. The fact is, if that liquid had been the same as used to dip millions of sheep and that handled by tens of thousands of farm workers every year, he could well have been maimed, whereas the only thing damaged by Sue's action was his pride.

Of course we didn't quite get away with it. At his visit for the second dipping, he noticed our two pigs Fred and Kinky. 'Where is your licence to bring pigs here?' he asked. I went to the office and fetched the two movement licences.

'Where did you get these,' he quizzed. I explained to him that we obtained them from the local police station. 'The issuing of licences for the movement of pigs has not been a police function for years,' he replied, shaping to slip the licences in his pocket. 'That's not our fault,' I said, grabbing them from his hand. And off he went to harass some unfortunate local police officer.

Within days yet another MAFF official arrived – this time a woman.

'I understand you have a cow,' she said, pulling on rubber boots and spraying them with disinfectant. I explained that we had indeed just accepted a Jersey heifer named Misty from a farm in Yeovil. She was nine months old, but was only half the size she should have been at that age. She had been ill since birth and her owner had spent a fortune in veterinary fees to try and cure her laboured breathing. Finally, they gave up and had it not been for our intervention Misty would have taken a one-way trip to the local Hunt kennels to be killed and fed to the hounds – the fate of around 400,000 dead or sick cows and calves every year.

We had heard about her through a friend and when we offered her a permanent home at Ferne the owners seemed relieved that there was an alternative to slaughter. We collected her, a stunted little calf, mucus dripping from her nose, and with a large solid lump of dry dung completely encasing the hairy tuft at the end of her tail. This lump was so heavy that she couldn't raise her tail when passing dung and thus the pendulum was constantly growing in size and weight from new dung deposits.

We had to use pliers to break away the solid mass from her tail, and washed it thoroughly with soapy water. When we had dried her she swished her tail from side to side, turning her head to see her new fly-whisk in operation. She danced a few steps, stopped to check that her tail was still following, then scampered over to the watching goats to show it off.

She was soon growing rapidly on a diet supplemented by garlic, sea-weed, parsley, watercress and a few vitamins and within a year had made up all her growth. Later she was joined by three more rescued cattle.

Not that Misty's rescue from slaughter or a life of exploitation interested the MAFF vet, of course. 'Where's your permit?' she snapped. 'Permit? What permit?' I queried. 'This is a Brucellosis Eradication Area and no animals are allowed in without a permit,' she replied as I groaned inwardly. She explained that she would have to go to Yeovil to check whether the farm where Misty had been reared was 'accredited'. If not, Misty would have to be subjected to tests which if positive would mean instant removal for

Misty in the snow

slaughter. After dropping that bomb-shell, she swapped her Wellingtons for shoes, jumped in her car and shot off up the drive – leaving us discussing whether we knew of any friends to whom we could smuggle Misty if her birth-place did not turn out to be accredited.

To our relief, later that the day the MAFF vet rang and confirmed that the Yeovil farm was 'accredited', 'But you must still obtain a permit,' she added. Then the letters started to arrive. 'Under article 16 of the Tuberculosis Order 1964 you have been allocated Herd Mark ZE668,' ordered the Ministry. 'All your bovine animals must have that number tattooed in the right ear or on a plastic tag fixed in a hole punched through the right ear,' droned the missive, adding that each animal must have its own number added to the herd number.

I rang to protest that we did not have a 'herd', but just one Jersey heifer, but an official insisted that one cow is a herd as far as they were concerned and that Misty would have to be tagged or tattooed. We were told that the only exception was a pedigree animal registered with a Breed Society. We made a few enquiries and to our pleasurable surprise we found that Misty had indeed been registered as a pedigree Jersey at birth. I rang MAFF to inform them of the position and asked whether we could consequently assume that Misty was no longer a 'herd'.

'Not that simple,' said an official. If we had a cow, we had a herd, even if the one cow was not a member of it! This was too good a silly season story not report to the media and so I rang the Western Daily Press and told them about MAFF's attempt to apply farming regulations to a pet cow. This particular paper was already conducting a long-running war against MAFF for its badger gassing programme and the next day the front page featured a super picture of Misty with a story ridiculing MAFF. We never heard another word about tattoos and tags and herd numbers from MAFF, even when we later added other cattle to the herd. However, the Ministry had not finished with us yet.

A couple of days later we received a questionnaire headed, 'We do not appear to have your "Holding Number" registered. Please fill in answers to the questions below.' I rang them, explained that we were not a farm, did not deal in animals, produce or crops and did not consider ourselves to be 'agricultural' in any way. Two days later I received a letter advising us that we were now 'Holding Number 36/167/37'!

The whole situation would have been funny had it not been for the fact that while MAFF was showering us with paperwork and sending a queue officials because we had two sheep, two pigs and one cow, there were millions and millions of farm livestock and poultry living miserable lives in intensive, disease-ridden conditions, abused in markets, transported long distances with no food water or rest, and brutally killed in fearful slaughterhouses.

A few years later when Misty was a fine, strong and extremely gentle cow, she had been joined by Maggie, a Friesian calf, a 17 year-old Jersey cow named Queenie and Muppet, a large-horned Guernsey steer. Queenie was unique. Her owner had farmed a dairy herd all his working life, but had the extraordinary record of never sending a cow for slaughter. He kept his cows well into old age and had them slaughtered on his farm when the time came. I have never come across such a caring livestock farmer before or since. He had retired from farming five years previously, but had kept his last cow, Queenie, as a pet, until he had to give up his farm and move to urban life in Exeter. His last act as a farmer was to load Queenie into a horse-box and bring her to Ferne. After satisfying himself that Ferne was ideal for her permanent retirement, he left with his eyes brimming with tears. He returned a year later to renew his friendship with her. Apart from trimming the ends of her horns occasionally because they turned back towards her eyes, she was no problem to care for. She was healthy, quiet and gentle; the complete opposite of Maggie!

Maggie arrived in the arms of a Polish farm labourer from a farm in Dorset. She had almost died at birth, but the Pole fought for her life day after day and night after night. His boss had predicted his efforts would be in vain and was so confident that the calf wouldn't survive, that he told the Pole that if he saved Maggie he could decide her future.

Little Maggie pulled through and when she was a couple of months old and fit and strong, her rescuer rang us and asked if she could become a permanent resident at Ferne; he had read about the sanctuary in a newspaper article. He and Maggie duly arrived, wrapped in blankets, having travelled in the cold on the open flat-back of a lorry for a journey of more than sixty miles. It was the only form of transport he could find. There are some wonderful people on this planet!

Unlike the gentle Misty, Queenie and Muppet, Maggie grew up to be a complete vandal. As far as she was concerned, everybody and everything existed to be chased, attacked and generally battered. She found the other cows and the horses boring; so she spent most of her time with the more playful goats and sheep. As a precaution against her causing injuries, we filed down the points of her horns, but this did not stop her worst vice; vandalising lorries! She would hear a lorry coming down the drive, and paw the ground with anticipation. When the vehicle came to a halt in the yard, she would attack it head down and smash the headlights with vicious thrusts of her horns. After we had paid out two big cheques for repairs, we had to ensure that she was locked behind a strong field-gate whenever we were expecting any deliveries of supplies.

One Sunday, visitors' day, I heard one of the staff give the alarm call, 'Grockles coming'. ['Grockle' is a highly disrespectful West Country term for a tourist. It always amused me when I saw tourists

Maggie the terror

innocently wandering into a tacky-souvenir shop called 'Grockles' in Lyme Regis. Friends of mine near Axminster so hated the summer visitors responsible for leaving litter in country lanes around their home that they had a car-sticker specially printed that read, 'Keep Britain Tidy – Shoot a Grockle Today!'] Anyone visiting the sanctuary had to park their vehicle in our top field and walk down the steep drive to the house and yard. The drive first descended the hill at an angle and then dog-legged along a horizontal track to the reception area in the main yard. That Sunday, we had seen three elderly ladies walking down the first part of the drive, but for some reason they didn't arrive in the yard. So, after waiting for a couple of minutes and thinking that they may have opened the wooden gate which was the private entrance to our staff's living quarters, I walked along the track to look for them. I soon found the reason for the delay.

Denis, the sanctuary's secretary, had parked his car at the bottom of the sloping drive and three elderly ladies were scampering around it pursued by a frisky Maggie. The ladies were terrified (and I don't blame them). They were red-faced and puffing on one side of the car, while Maggie snorted at them from the other. Then as Maggie bucked excitedly and dashed around their side, the ladies quickly swapped places with her. Next the ladies were at the front with Maggie peering at them through the rear windscreen, then a quick scuffle and everyone changed positions.

I ran to the rescue, shouting and waving my arms at Maggie and driving her along the track towards the yard, shouting to one of the staff to shut her in the goats' paddock. Returning to the ladies to offer profuse apologies, I found that they were already walking quickly back up the drive to the car park! I walked alongside them all the way to the top, offering my sincerest apologies and trying to convince them that Maggie was just being playful and that she was now safely confined if they would like to have a guided tour around the sanctuary. But it was too late. They were scarlet with indignation and humiliation and in no mood to accept my grovelling expressions of regret. I held the gate open for them as they drove out; all three staring straight ahead and ignoring my wave of contrition.

There were, however, some people who positively deserved Maggie's harassment. I'm not ashamed to say that we used Maggie to get our revenge for all the hassle we had suffered from officials of the dreaded Ministry of Agriculture. A man arrived one day to tell us that he had been instructed to collect blood samples from all our cattle so that they could be tested for Brucellosis. In his late forties, and clearly from a farming background, he was a short, stocky, strong looking man. He explained that he was contracted by MAFF to visit farms and collect blood samples. He'd 'done thousands,' he informed us.

He showed us his identification and explained that he would

take the blood either from the neck or the tail, that it was very quick and painless. I told him that we considered the procedure was a complete waste of time and tax-payers' money, but that we would bring the four animals into a paddock at the front of the stables, and the rest was up to him.

We got Misty, Queenie, Muppet and Maggie into the paddock by offering them some food in buckets, then slid the rails across to enclose the four animals. The word quickly went around the sanctuary and within a few minutes all seven of us staff were leaning on the paddock rails. It was like a scene from an old western where trail-wise cowboys gather round a paddock to watch a 'green-horn' try to ride some a notorious, crazy, unbroken stallion. Give the man his due, within 20 minutes he had got a head-collar onto Misty, Queenie and Muppet, tied them to posts, and deftly collected his blood-samples with a syringe. He led each of them in turn to the fence slid back the rails and turned them back into the field.

Only Maggie was left to deal with. My conscience suddenly pricked me, and I shouted to him, 'Watch out for Maggie; she's a bit difficult.' He nodded an acknowledgement as he shook a bucket of nuts and maize at Maggie. He had first draped a headcollar over the bucket so that as she thrust her nose into the bucket her head would be in the collar. He lowered the bucket to the ground so that her head was deep inside, her tongue rasping the food in the bottom. If he had just pulled the collar tight and hung onto the rope, he might have got away with it, but he made the mistake of grasping one of her horns in one hand as he pulled the collar tight with the other. The next thing he knew he was sitting in the mud on the other side of the paddock fence. Maggie had simply thrust her head upwards and dumped him right over the top rail.

Trying not to laugh out loud, we continued to watch as he dusted himself off and clambered back into the paddock. While we discussed the odds against him ever completing his task, he advanced on Maggie again, bucket in one hand, head collar in the other. Several times he tried to capture her as she bucked, twisted, turned and charged around the paddock. Several times he suffered defeat; either from being barged against the fence or being dragged through the mud at the end of a rope She thought it was a terrific game. How great to find a human being who enjoyed such games!

It was only when she finally got bored with the whole thing that he managed to tie her to a post and get his precious blood-sample. It had taken him nearly an hour and we gave him an appreciative round of applause as with sweat dripping from his brow he pulled on his coat, closed up his bag and strode trium-phantly back to his car in the yard. He never came to the sanctuary again. And thereafter Maggie had to content herself with scrapping with the goats.

Rodents and Rabbits

The first rabbit to arrive at the new Ferne was simply named 'Bun'. He was large with blue/grey fur and arrived with his friend, a guinea-pig, with which he had shared a tiny hutch for years. We had not yet built facilities for rabbits and guinea pigs, but we had cleared out a rickety old hay barn that consisted of nothing more than a tin roof fixed at the top of six telegraph poles. We made it into a day pen for Bun and his friend by nailing wire netting around the six poles, and provided a bigger hutch for night quarters. The freedom had a dramatic effect on Bun. Once released into the pen, he dashed crazily around, leaping high into the air, squirting urine in all directions. Unfortunately he also started to become really aggressive with his guinea-pig friend – so aggressive that we had to separate them.

We decided that the best place for Bun was the cattery where he had a huge garden to run around, plenty of grass and bushes to nibble and, if he wished, could even dig his own burrow. The problem was that, having been deprived of a guinea pig to push around, he decided to bully the cats. He raced around inside the cattery leaping into baskets and cardboard boxes, turfing out cats and chasing them so aggressively that they were forced to find refuge on shelves. We thought that things would settle down in a few days, but Bun brought things to a head when he made the mistake of trying to push old Tabatha out of her basket. Tabatha, deaf and elderly, and a former Australian stray, was the boss of the cattery, but she was oblivious to Bun causing mayhem around her as she dozed contentedly. Suddenly Bun leapt into her basket, probably assuming she would react like the other cats and leap for safety. Not Tabatha. She awoke in a flash and smacked Bun straight in the eye with a razor sharp claw. As soon as we realised the extent of his injury we bundled him into a box and whipped him down to our local veterinary surgery, but despite treatment he eventually lost his sight in the damaged eye.

Once he had recovered, we tried to introduce him to a couple of newly rescued rabbits, but his aggression was undiminished. After much discussion we decided to offer him the freedom of the entire sanctuary. He loved it. He would hop around during the day following staff members going about their work. He enjoyed the company of the goats and seemed to have the sense not to try his pushing them around. One day he was not seen around all day, but in the evening, when I was returning from checking the active badger setts on our neighbour's land, Bun suddenly hopped out of the bushes to greet me. However, he didn't accompany me home and had clearly chosen to become a wild rabbit. He was only spotted a couple of times after that; I hope he didn't decide to go down a badger sett or fox earth to try and evict the residents!

There once was a man who for some reason best known to himself purchased a python. The pet-shop owner told him that it wouldn't want to eat very often and that the best way to find out when it was hungry was to offer it a live rat (which the pet shop could supply of course!) So a week or so after settling the snake into its vivarium, the man went to the pet shop and bought a rat. He took it home and put it into the tank with the python, whereupon the snake opened an eye, yawned and went back to sleep. The man took the rat out, bought a cage to keep it in and decided that he would keep it for a week and then offer it to the python again. The trouble was that he found the rat much more interesting and friendly than the python and when the time came to offer it again to the python for a meal, he couldn't bear to do it! So he went to the pet shop and bought another rat that he didn't know.

He put the new rat into the snake's tank – but once again the python wasn't interested. So the first rat got a pal! A couple of weeks later yet another rat was purchased; and once again the python declined. The two rats became three, and so it went on with new facilities being built for the growing rat tribe. Inevitably, the pet shop wrongly identified the sex of a rat and soon the family of rats were doing their own multiplication. Then after the best part of a year with the python preferring to sleep rather than eat, the man decided to end the nightmare by donating the snake to a zoo and asking us to take what by then was a colony of 53 rats.

We converted part of our food-bin shed into two large pens to separate the males and females, installed pipes as tunnels, tree stumps and branches to climb on, and shelves on which the rats could sit and groom themselves and look out at the world. They became a major attraction for the visitors and even featured on Westward Television. Their presence (and some sloppy sweeping round the food bins) attracted wild rats to the shed. We found ourselves in the somewhat illogical situation of spending sanctuary funds feeding and caring for 53 tame rats, while trying to deprive wild rats of food and setting a cage-trap to capture them for transfer to some woods a long way from the sanctuary.

Every night we baited the traps with food; and every morning the food was still there and the traps empty. This went on for several days until one morning the cage was filled to bursting with seven large brown rats. It seems that once one rat braved the suspicious cage, the rest rushed in too. They were quickly taken to the woods and released; whether they made their way back to the sanctuary I don't know, but no rat ever entered the trap again.

After we had removed the remaining wild rats' food source by enforcing strict rules of hygiene around the food bins, they quickly found another ready supply.

They moved under the row of six small sheds which served as rabbit and guinea-pigs accommodation. Each hut contained three or four rabbits and a couple of guinea pigs. Once a day we placed a bowl of maize, bran and oats in each of the six outside grass runs and the rabbits and guinea-pigs would squat around their bowl to feed. As soon as the staff member was out of sight, a small group of rats scampered out from under the sheds, pushed their noses between the rabbits and guinea-pigs, and having shouldered their way in, happily helped themselves. As soon as we realised what was happening we had to make sure rabbit feeding time was supervised and the bowls and any spilt food removed afterwards.

The wild rats were not always a nuisance. In the house we had one large room for the ten or twelve 'yardies', dogs which were unlikely due to age or looks to find a new home and which were safe with the wide variety of animals and birds wandering free in the sanctuary. Sleeping beds and baskets filled with shredded newspaper were dotted around the otherwise plain room. Every morning we threw open the double door and the lot of them would rush out into the old orchard shrieking and barking to greet the new day.

Most of them would defecate in the orchard either then or shortly after their daily meal, and it was not the most pleasant of chores to wander round the orchard with a bucket to collect up the faeces and take it to the incinerator.

One hectic day, due to a couple of veterinary emergencies, the daily orchard clean-up had been left. At dusk I happened to be in the office looking out at the orchard, when I saw a movement. I watched fascinated as wild rats began to appear from all directions, rush out into the grass, grab a dog 'turd' and rush back under cover. Most took their 'prizes' under a large pile of old branches, sticks and hedge cuttings at the end of the orchard, where presumably they sorted through them for undigested bits of food. It reminded me of a story I had read somewhere, that claimed that were it not for the rats sorting through and breaking up jams in the bends of London's sewers, the streets of London would be flooded with sewage. Bearing in mind the constant use of countless tons of poison placed in the sewers to kill rats, I suppose the story is little more than an urban myth. However, from then on we were happy to hand over the daily orchard 'dog-turd' collection to the sanctuary's wild rat population!

One of the most intelligent rodents we had the pleasure of accommodating was Gerald the 'bionic' gerbil. He had been brought in after being found with a broken leg. That soon mended, but as neither Sue nor I could stand seeing animals in cages, we gave Gerald the run of the house. It's amazing just how quickly one becomes used to sharing with such a tiny rodent. Often, while going upstairs, one would meet Gerald on his way down, or vice versa. In the evening when we flopped into armchairs to watch television, Gerald would crawl through a gap under the door, climb up onto an arm of the chair, gently take a nut from between one's lips and sit there nibbling his TV snack!

Until Gerald moved in, we had always had problems with mice.

The old thatched farmhouse was ideal habitat for house-mice and I caught dozens in cage traps and transferred them to the stables. Gerald built several food caches around the house – behind the Aga, under the fridge and under the lounge floor boards. To stop the mice stealing his food, Gerald constantly patrolled the house terrorising and beating up any mouse he found. Finally, there was only one mouse which had not fled from the house, a very old and extremely tame little chap who would climb up onto the kitchen table and search for crumbs while we were eating breakfast.

Gerald made his life a misery and whenever he came across him there would be a high speed chase around the kitchen floor, a skirmish under the fridge and a nose to tail sprint out through the hall – the mouse squeaking in terror. The old mouse, the edges of his ears increasingly tattered, continued to appear on the kitchen table every day, until one day he climbed the kitchen window curtains, walked along the pelmet and fell dead onto the table!

Gerald continued his patrols and we noticed that often he disappeared for hours under the airing cupboard door in the first floor bathroom. One day I decided to see where he lived and lifted a floor board, to find a huge white nest made out of fluff from the bathroom carpet. To my horror I saw that two electric cables ran right through the centre of the nest and that Gerald had nibbled off all the insulation from both cables over a length of several inches.

I rushed to turn off the electric supply – shaking in the knowledge that at any time we could have been burnt in our beds in the rambling, thatched farmhouse, four miles from the nearest fire-station and without any mains water supply. After calling in an electrician to replace the stripped wires and check the system, we captured Gerald and confined him to a specially constructed sandy mini-environment. As soon as Gerald was off the scene, more mice moved in – and we had to resort to the cage trap and the daily trip to the stables.

I must have carried scores of mice in the small cage-trap, five or six at a time, the 150 yards to the stables. One of the stables was used to store best quality hay and another to store bales of poly-thene-wrapped bales of wood shavings which we used as bedding in the large field shelter constantly open to the horses. I tipped each consignment of house-mice into the shavings store where they scampered off amongst the bales. The staff often taunted me about these regular trips, teasingly claiming that the mice were returning to the house at night and that therefore I was probably carrying the same half a dozen mice every trip.

As the weeks went by, we gradually used up the bales of shavings and none of the stable staff saw any sign of the mice. I had decided to switch to shredded newspaper as it was cheaper and less dusty, and gave instructions that we should empty the store completely before we re-filled it with bales of newspaper. It was my turn to clean out the field shelter and put down the last of the woodshavings. As I cut the strings holding the last bale together, it suddenly fell in half, revealing a core consisting of a large, round, greyish-brown sphere. The ball was a huge ball of live mice whose members, suddenly realising they were exposed, exploded around the stable squeaking in panic. Rapidly gaining their bearings they shot out through the open doorway and scampered under the door of the next stable to safely amongst the hay bales.

So we had learned that the mice captured in the house had stayed where they were put, had built themselves a nice cosy communal home in a bale of shavings, and no doubt popped next door to feed off the grass seeds and other delicacies in the hay store. And for the more adventurous of them it was only about thirty yards along the concrete apron of the stables to the food store where there were always a few bits of bran, oats and maize spilt from filling the horses' feed buckets. Fearing contamination of the hay, we removed most of it to our hay-loft on the yard, leaving the mice a few bales on which to live.

With Gerald's mouse-mugging days over, he was joined in his special gerbil house by more rescued gerbils. Two had been found abandoned in a coal bunker and another four adults complete with cage were left over at the end of a closing-down sale of a local pet shop. While we were checking the sexes of the four we found six tiny babies snuggled up in the nest. The pet shop owner didn't even know of their existence, so it was just as well he hadn't managed to sell the mother, or her young would have starved to death.

I have hated pet shops ever since in the early 1970s in Dorset, I had passed one on a Sunday and saw two Mynah birds in a cage.

One bird was cowering and bleeding in the corner as the other periodically jumped down from its perch and set about it with its beak. Being a Sunday the shop was closed and so I went to the local police station only yards away to ask for action to be taken to rescue the victim before it was killed. An officer invited me to ring the RSPCA, but I refused – pointing out that a criminal offence of neglect was taking place and that I expected the police to deal with criminal offences. The embarrassed police officer confided in me that the pet shop was in fact owned by the Chairman of the local magistrates bench.

The officer seemed surprised when I told him that I was not interested in who owned the shop and I insisted on the shop being opened. Eventually after taking advice, the shop owner was contacted by telephone and he agreed to come to the shop and separate the birds. What sort of pet shop owner does not even know that two mynah birds should never be kept together in a small cage?

A couple of weeks later I visited the shop again – when it was open. On the forecourt of the shop was a large slatted packing-case full of newly imported tortoises (this was before the importation of tortoises had been banned). A few limp lettuces had been thrown in with them and I stood watching for a while until I realised that one of the animals was not moving. I looked closer and saw that it was dead. As I peered even closer a stench hit my nostrils and I saw a maggot emerge from its eye. In fact it was crawling with maggots and clearly had been dead for days.

I angrily marched into the shop and as loudly as I could, asked an assistant, 'Why are you selling dead tortoises?' Everything went quiet as the two or three customers stopped talking. I repeated the question and a woman I took to be the manageress came from the back of the shop. 'Can I help you?' she asked angrily. I pointed out, again as loudly as I could, that there was a crate of tortoises outside for sale, one of which was not only dead, but crawling with maggots. We marched outside and I pointed to the rotten tortoise. As a crowd began to form, the manageress poked it with a stick which exposed more maggots and a fresh waft of disgusting stench. 'It was all right this morning,' whined the woman, to which the small crowd joined me in a collective; 'Pah'. Red-faced, she disappeared into the shop and emerged with a spade with which she removed the putrid creature and holding the corpse as far out in front as possible disappeared out the back of the shop. The whole farce was worthy of rivalling the Monty Python 'dead parrot' sketch!

I don't think pet shops should be permitted to sell any live creatures at all. They are responsible for perpetuating the concept of live animals being 'things' to buy on impulse; they encourage the terrible trade in exotic birds, animals, fish and insects which should be left in their natural habitats, and they thrive on selling animals like hamsters and rabbits, and birds such as canaries and budgerigars which usually spend their entire lives in cages. And such shops are usually run by people who have no training in animal care – particularly of exotic creatures. If possible, those of us with pets should try to avoid buying any food or other pet supplies from shops which also sell animals.

Horses and Ponies

Before I went to Ferne, equines of any sort were an unknown quantity as far as I was concerned. Fortunately Sue had years of experience in stables and owned her own pony which she eventually transported to Ferne from Essex.

I found the size of horses intimidating, mainly because if you are watching their teeth you can't see their feet and vice versa. The previous manager of Ferne didn't exactly enhance my confidence when he explained that the leader of the herd, a fifteen-year old pure-bred Connemara named Lady Patricia, was so wild that two or three times a year, a marksman from Longleat Safari Park had to be called in to shoot her with a tranquilliser dart and render her completely unconscious – merely to trim her hooves!

We immediately resolved to bring that ridiculous situation to an end. Upon reading the history of the seven horses resident at Ferne when we took over its management, we learned that Lady Patricia (or Patsy) had been born in the sanctuary when it was stationed at the old Ferne Estate near Shaftesbury.

Patsy's mother had been brought in for a temporary stay at the sanctuary when her owner was seriously ill. By the time the owner recovered sufficiently from her long illness to recover her mare, Patsy had been born, and the owner agreed to allow her to remain free at the sanctuary for life.

At the old Ferne Estate the horses and ponies had more than a hundred acres of pasture to roam in, but clearly the previous staff neglected to spend sufficient time winning their friendship and trust. Most of the horses had spent years being ridden or worked by human beings and although some had been abused and nervous, they were at least reasonably handleable. This did not apply to

Lady Patricia. In her entire life she had never been saddled, never had a bit in her mouth and not even felt a bridle or head collar. She was as near a wild horse one can find in a domestic situation.

Within a few months, by spending as much time daily with the herd as possible, running a hand along Patsy's back or down her leg, offering titbits, and gradually winning her trust, we eventually progressed to momentarily picking-up a front foot and then to holding it up and picking out the mud with a hoof-pick. Try as we might, however, she would never tolerate a head collar or bridle. As soon as the dreaded item appeared, she would snort and move off, calling her herd to follow. The only way to keep her feet trimmed was to offer her a handful of pony nuts, lift a foot, clean it out the hoof and try a bit of trimming, before she stamped her foot down again. Then she had to be soothed again, offered a few more

Patricia leads her herd on patrol

nuts in the hope of doing a little more work on her feet. Consequently it often took several days to make sure all her feet were neat and tidy. The first time we picked up her back feet I was really worried that she might lash out, but although she was uneasy about the indignity, she never kicked. She always gave us plenty of warning that she had enough by waving her foot about to break one's grip, and put it back on the ground. If she was in the right mood, she would permit us to lift the foot again to complete the trimming. If she was not in the mood, then it was time to put the tools away until another day.

Including Patsy, there were only seven horses and ponies at Ferne when we arrived, but once we had built new stables and a large field shelter we gradually built the numbers up to twenty. They ranged in size from little Joey, a 30-year-old Exmoor pony

Big Patrick

rescued from life on a chain, to big Patrick, a 32-year-old Clydesdale cart-horse retired from a life of pulling farm equipment. [Incidentally, Joey died in 1998 aged 52 – the oldest known pony in Britain at the time.]

I rapidly became fascinated with Ferne's equine family. Many a warm night we would walk out across the fields to find the herd and spend an hour or two just sitting on the hill amongst them in the darkness. They were moments of true peace and relaxation – the only sounds being grass being ripped from the turf by a score of sets of teeth, the occasional slap and slop of wet dung onto mud, a cough or two, or an itchy rump being rasped on a gate-post.

Little Joey

Lady Patricia remained as herd leader – some unseen quality preserving her status despite her herd being trebled in size. Maybe it was her unbroken spirit, her straight, unbowed back which no human had ever straddled.

Her leadership was dramatically demonstrated within weeks of our arrival. The first task of every new day was to walk out into the fields to find the horses and donkeys and make sure they were all alive and well. One morning the herd was grazing in the bottom field, but away from the rest one of them lay stone dead. It was Jason, a hunter in his twenties, who according to his record card had never been the fittest of the bunch due to a weak heart. From the signs, he had dropped dead in his tracks. For example there was little disturbance of the turf around him, and that indicated that he had not been flailing his feet around in pain or scrabbling to get to his feet. As we crouched examining Jason's body, the rest of the herd continued to graze, seemingly totally disinterested. This didn't surprise me as Jason always seemed slightly apart from the rest of the herd. He was always last in the queue when the members of the herd were vying for the best places in the field shelter in rainy weather, a clear indication that he was the lowest in the herd's pecking order.

We decided to move the horses out of the field and shut the gate to keep them out of the way when the knacker's yard vehicle came to collect the body. The vehicle could gain access through another gate that led from a rough farm track. We walked back to stables, half-filled several buckets with pony nuts and set them out in a row. Sue then repeatedly called to the horses, a long drawn out 'Keeem-on. Keeem-on. Patsy, Patsy.' Within seconds the herd was charging excitedly up the hill towards us led by Patricia and accompanied by much snorting and whinnying, and followed by the equally excited donkeys. Soon they were all heads down in the buckets, ears back and rumps swinging from side to side, defending their food. Then Sue set off down the field to close the gate, but she had only gone a few yards when Patricia lifted her head from her bucket, looked along the line of noisily chomping ponies and neighed loudly causing every head to emerge from the row of black rubber buckets. Then she turned and galloped furiously back down the field they had only just left, quickly followed by the thundering hooves of the rest of her herd. She led them in single file through the gate and towards Jason's prone body that Patricia eyed and sniffed suspiciously. Then the entire herd silently circled the body, each of them raising and lowering their heads as they smelled death. Thus they stood for a full twenty minutes in what appeared to be a silent tribute to their lost herd member.

Then, the 'ceremony' over, Patricia led the herd back through the gate, away to a far part of the sanctuary's 36 acres – their food forgotten – to go about their business. After that day, whenever we had to destroy one of the equine family due to sickness or injury we always made sure it was done in the presence of the rest of the herd and that the body remained accessible to them for twenty four hours. For too long too many of us have accepted the Victorian anthropomorphic view that no animal should be slaughtered within sight of its kin. Indeed that is still the rule in our slaughter-houses. To comply with this, each herd animal, whether it be pig, sheep or cow, has to be physically separated from its herd-mates. Following this alien and frightening experience, each animal is then driven into a clanking, confusing world of metal and concrete, strange smells and unknown, impatient men on a piece-work system. Thus every single animal destroyed in our slaughter-houses is under great stress. It need not be so.

I once discussed the slaughter of animals with a man who had spent some time in India demonstrating captive-bolt humane killers donated by animal welfare societies to native cattle slaughters who hitherto had clubbed the animals to death with pole-axes. He explained to me that firstly he tied the cattle by halters to a fence. Then as the animals munched hay, he walked along the line killing each animal with a single shot in the brain. He said that done this way there was no panic and that the animals were only aware that the cow next to them suddenly lay down. The fact that their kin were being killed was beyond their comprehension and therefore they felt no fear. Compare this with the stress suffered by animals transported long distances, separated from their kind and driven alone and terrified into a tiny space in which they are shot.

Another myth is that animals become terrified at the sight or smell of blood. This is complete nonsense. I remember two occasions when horses had to be shot by our veterinary surgeons at

Ferne. Both had been ill and had been confined to a stable for treatment. When the vet recommended destruction, the animals were shot inside their stables and the doors thrown open for the rest of the herd to wander in if they wished. Once we had retired from the scene Patricia would wander in along the apron to peer into the open stable to see and sniff the body. Then the rest would follow so that soon there were horses in and around the body, sniffing for a few minutes then wandering out for another to take their place.

When an animal is shot in the brain it drops as fast as the blink of an eye. Blood pours out of the nostrils and a large pool spreads around the body. I have seen the entire herd of horses, followed by several curious donkeys, step in and around the blood without the slightest indication of unease.

The fact is that animals are not frightened of the smell of blood. What generates fear and distress are unusual events, strange noises, humans shouting, sticks waving and most of all separation from their kind. Blood and death mean nothing to them.

I became more and more intrigued with horses. Every time a new horse arrived at the sanctuary – not always old, but often ill-treated – it was always a signal for the staff to drop what they were doing. The new arrivals would step out of their horse-boxes into the yard with ears pricked, anxiously looking around their new surroundings. After a quick check, we would throw open the gate into the fields and send them through to meet their new companions with whom they would spend the rest of their lives.

Sometimes the newcomer would be bold, and trot confidently towards the herd – which would raise a collective head from grazing and move excitedly towards the newcomer. Often Patricia would step out ahead of the herd, head and tail high, to get the first sniff of the 'intruder'. Usually there was great excitement, tossing of heads, snorts and neighs, ears back, teeth bared, rumps swinging, back legs lashing the air, followed by frantic bursts of galloping in different directions. But on other occasions, the arrival and acceptance of a new herd member would cause hardly a flicker of excitement. The animal would just mingle in and begin grazing as if it had been at Ferne all its life. Soon its place in the pecking order would become established. It would be nothing to with size, age or breed, but depended on some hidden dominance factor – and rarely established by any display of force or aggression.

With my new-found knowledge of horses came a new respect. Studying a herd of horses unfettered, unsaddled, no metal bits in their mouths and no reins and harnesses, is fascinating. Even though most of Ferne's equines were pensioners, they still loved to gallop at the slightest excuse. A plastic bag flying across the field in the wind could provoke a reaction one would normally consider appropriate for the arrival of some hungry predator. Patsy would squeal and stamp and within seconds the entire herd would be whirling and galloping, heads tossing and hind legs kicking and lashing out behind them as they thundered from field to field. It became obvious that they knew full well that they were not really in any danger and that they were inventing fright, just as children will do playing 'ghosts' or 'monsters'.

We worked a rotation system in order to always keep one field shut off from the horses and the rest of the grazing animals. This not only enabled us to take a cut of hay every summer, but also provided the fun of calling the horses to the field, throwing the gate open and watching them excitedly charging into the 'new' territory. Led by Patricia, with their ears pricked, they would gallop around the field and then throw themselves down to roll on the turf. Even when most of the horses had been at Ferne for years and knew every inch of the sanctuary, each time they were given access to a field which had been shut off to them for months they treated it as if it was a completely new and exciting territory.

Learning what depths there are to horses and their ways made me more sad about the exploitation to which they have been subjected by man. What a shame that their physiology ever suited them for our use. Where would human beings be now if it were not for horses? How far would we have ever traveled if it were not for horses carrying or pulling us? How many millions of horses have been slashed, speared, shot or blown to pieces in our stupid human wars? How dare we still expose them to danger in human conflicts such as riots and demonstrations? How dare we take advantage of their joy of galloping with their kind, and put their limbs and lives at risk in spectacles like the Grand National where even when exhausted they are whipped because some human wants to win some money and a stupid cup? And worst of all, how dare we pervert their strength, speed and stamina to help us entertain ourselves hounding some fox or deer to exhaustion and death?

Horse exploiters are just the most nauseating and hypocritical of all animal users. Owners, trainers and jockeys stand brazenly in front of a television camera and say how 'devastated' they are at the death of their horse because it had to be shot after breaking a leg in a race. Yet they knew full well before they entered their horse in the event that many horses have died previously at such races. I remember once watching a video-tape of a dog-fighter crying because his pit-bull terrier had been killed in a fight in which he had not only willingly entered his dog, but had also placed a sizeable wager. People who put their animals into situations where it is obvious that they may suffer and die, have no right to claim distress They deserve prosecution for cruelty – not sympathy.

At Ferne we occasionally came across horse and pony owners who did have a conscience. George was a seven year old Skewbald pony. He had a pleasant disposition, but was suffering from navicular disease – ulceration of the navicular bone in the foot originally sparked off by an injury. Severe pain can result from the flexor tendon rubbing on the ulcerated bone and is generally considered amongst veterinarians as incurable. Usually the only alternative to humane destruction is surgically severing the nerves in the foot so that the animal is free from pain. The problem with this option is that without the ability to suffer pain, the horse can suffer terrible damage from stones or other sharp objects becoming embedded in the foot. One vet told us that he had once seen a horse with a de-nerved foot so severely damaged that it had dropped off.

George's owners could not face having him destroyed, but neither did they want to take the drastic step of having him de-nerved. We agreed to accept him at Ferne where we hoped complete rest might ease the condition. He arrived lame and in some pain. Taking advice from an experienced farrier, we pared his hoof to give more support, kept his hoof clear of stones and mud by checking several times a day, and put him on a high dose of comfrey tablets. Comfrey is known to herbalists as a great healer of bones – indeed one of its old country names is 'knit-bone'. Within two months George had lost all signs of lameness and as a comparative youngster was one of the livelier members of the herd.

However, the following winter when the ground was hardened by frost, the local Hunt decided to meet nearby and canter along the road which formed the sanctuary's north boundary. Why they met on such a day I don't know, and they soon abandoned the hunt due to the dangerously hard conditions underfoot. But their canter along the road so excited our horses and ponies that they galloped backwards and forwards alongside the hedge neighing at the horses and their green and black coated riders.

Later that day George was lame again and clearly in a lot of pain. We assumed his navicular trouble had returned and brought him into a stable for the night. In the morning, as he was thoroughly miserable and could not put his foot to the ground, we called out our local vet and he advised keeping George stabled on straw for a few days. The following week with George still in pain and virtually on three legs our vet arrived with portable X-ray equipment. George's pastern (the part of the leg immediately above the hoof and below the fetlock joint) was very swollen and rock-hard. The X-ray revealed bone cancer in and around the sesamoid bone – a tiny bone at the back of the fetlock joint. The vet shrugged his shoulders; 'Nothing I can do,' he pronounced. 'It's euthanasia, I'm afraid.' 'That's interesting,' he added, looking closely at the X-rays again. 'There's no sign of that previous navicular disease at all.' So if the herbal remedy had worked before, why not on George's new problem? Our vet was in no doubt about the right course of action. 'He really is in a lot of pain. There's no cure – it's not fair to allow him to suffer any longer.'

Sue and I had a quick conference. We asked the vet if would supply us with enough Butazoladine – powerful painkiller to give George a week or so without so that we could pack his last few days with plenty of treats and extra affection. Our vet suggested that we should pick up some 'Bute' from his surgery in Axminster and that we should arrange for George to be euthanised the following week. We collected the 'Bute', stirred the odourless and tasteless powder into a bowl of cereals and offered it to George. He sniffed the bowl, but refused to eat. We then offered him another bowl of food without the powder and he scoffed the lot!

We tried all sorts of tempting dishes, and even crushed some peppermints into the bowl, but George would not accept anything containing the 'Bute'. Was this the end? How could we justify keeping a three-legged horse in pain, particularly as our vet had virtually insisted on euthanasia. Sue and I returned to the kitchen

George treated with flower remedies

to ponder the dilemma over a cup of tea. It was then that I remembered a leaflet which had arrived in the post some days previously. It was about the work of a spiritual healer in Saltash, Cornwall who met regularly with a group of friends in a 'healing circle' for sick humans ... and animals. I rummaged round in the office and found the leaflet which contained 'before and after' pictures of a domestic rabbit allegedly cured of terrible injuries.

Now there is no-one more cynical than me about the paranormal or miraculous, but we were desperate. After making a few phone calls, I found myself talking to Marilyn in Saltash who had a glorious Devonshire accent and sounded reassuringly 'normal'. I explained George's problem and asked whether there was anything she could do. 'Oh yes m'dear,' she sang. 'I'll put him on my list. Our circle is meeting tonight. He'll be all right.'

'Do you need a photograph or anything?' I asked.

'Only if you want to send me one. But we don't need one. Oh, and I'll put some Bach Flower Remedies in the post to you,' said Marilyn before ringing off with a cheerful 'Bye'.

I looked at Sue. 'She's going to put George on her list for healing,' I muttered. 'And she's sending us some flower remedies or something.'

'That's good,' said Sue unquestioningly. As a herbalist she was 'into all that sort of thing' anyway.

The next morning, I went out to the stables to check on George. I was amazed. He was gingerly testing his foot on the floor and looked bright and alert, and eager to get out into the field to the rest of the herd. The next day a Jiffy bag arrived in the post containing a small dropper bottle. Hand-written instructions explained that the bottle contained a combination of Bach Flower Remedies and that George should have four drops in food three times a day and two drops in his drinking water. We were also instructed to dilute three drops in water and dab the solution onto his injured leg four times a day.

Within days George was out of his stable and using his leg normally, although the thickened pastern somewhat restricted the flexibility of his lower leg leaving him slightly lame for the rest of his life. But this was of no concern as long as he was not in pain and could muster up a gallop with the rest of the herd. We continued with the course of flower remedies, although I must admit I felt ridiculous wandering the fields at night to find George so that I could dab his leg with a piece of cotton wool soaked in water containing nothing but a few drops from a bottle of distilled flower petals!

After two months we asked our vet to come back with his X-ray equipment. He was amazed to see George fit and well and even more amazed when the X-rays revealed that the bone disease was completely dead. When we explained that the treatment George had received consisted of absent spiritual healing and a few homeopathic doses of flower petals steeped in water, we could see from his face that he was having difficulty grasping the concept. Had it not been for the fact that he was in possession of X-rays showing both the existence and non-existence of the bone cancer, I'm sure he would have thought we were insane. As it was, he subsequently showed a real interest in alternative remedies and hopefully, wherever he is now, is using such wonders to compliment his own scientifically based knowledge and skills.

Many readers will have noticed Bach Flower Remedies in conventional chemist shops. They work on the principle that physical healing is hampered by 'dis-ease' of the mind. The flower remedies correct imbalances in the personality and free one's energies to deal with physical ailments. Following the success with George, we called for Marilyn's help on several occasions – especially with wild birds. Bach's 'rescue remedy' was particularly effective in combating shock – the biggest single killer of birds brought injured into wildlife hospitals. Another spectacular success was in healing a cat with leukaemia. After a short course of flower remedies the cat's condition rapidly improved. It put on weight and went on to live a long healthy life. Blood tests proved both that the cat was suffering from leukaemia and, following treatment, that it was clear of the disease.

The Ferne herd was an odd bunch. Patrick, the Clydesdale 'gentle giant', towered over truculent little Silver, a former riding school pony. Silver had been retired at the age of 30 from years of boredom carrying children round a paddock while they kicked him in the ribs and yanked his mouth about, took his revenge on the human race by making life awkward for us. Stubborn as the day was long, Silver made clear his objections to his feet being trimmed, by kicking out as soon as a hind foot was lifted. When we defeated him by refusing to let go of his airborne and wayward foot, he would appear to submit, but then when one was bent over double snipping and rasping away the excess hoof-growth, he would just lean on you to turn the task into a truly back-breaking exercise.

When he first came to Ferne he endeared himself to the other horses by demonstrating a trick he must have learned at his previous home. His trick was to use his rump to lift a gate off its hinges and thereby let the entire herd plus donkeys, cows and sheep into a field full of lush grass that we were keeping as a crop of hay. It took three of us an hour to drive them all out of the field and wire up the hinges to prevent Silver repeating his trick. The next day, we were amused to see Silver vigorously rubbing his rump up and down the hinge end of the gate, with the rest of the herd queuing up patiently waiting for access to the good grazing. Eventually Silver gave up and the horses wandered off – probably muttering under their breath about Silver's incompetence! It is almost certain that he originally learned the trick from rubbing an itchy rump on a gate and inadvertently lifting it off its hinges.

Silver was very much a grumpy old man and had no particular pal in the herd – until, that is, Sue's own horse, Smoky – a big strong Welsh cross cob, came down from Essex. Silver was slower and stiffer than the rest and was often left behind when the herd moved off to another field. Smoky would wait for him, chivvying him along with soft whinnies and was never far away from his side.

Then there was Mac, short for Macaroni, a pretty and tiny 10 hand four year old. His owners could no longer keep him, but they were vague about his history. They gave us the name of the dealers from whom they purchased him, but when we made enquiries they were very evasive and we even wondered whether he had been stolen. The reason we needed to know his background was that appeared not to have been gelded, and the last thing we needed was a stallion fathering even more ponies on the sanctuary. One testicle was visible, but we didn't know whether the other had been removed, whether it was still up inside him, or indeed whether he was even born with two! Our vets could easily remove the visible testicle, but finding out whether there was another that had failed to drop would need an expensive exploratory operation – probably at a veterinary hospital.

Our local vets booked Mac into Langford Teaching Hospital at Bristol, but told us that Langford would want to keep him in for ten days. We made our own enquiries and found a veterinary practice in Beaminster only 25 miles away that could carry out the operation in a specially equipped surgery. So we cancelled the Langford appointment and took little Mac to Beaminster. The vets there were superb. Including anaesthetists, there were seven vets waiting for what could be a tricky operation. Sue and I were allowed to attend, but the whole affair turned out to be a huge anti-climax. Mac was knocked out with halothane gas and as soon as he was turned over, there, clearly showing under the skin was the missing article! The operation was quickly performed and Mac was put into a nice clean stable for the night on a deep straw bed. The next day we drove down to collect him and he was soon back with the herd as if nothing had happened.

The only slight problem was that our local veterinary practice were annoyed with us for cancelling the Langford arrangement and they had insisted on being present at Beaminster to observe the operation. As it happened they did not turn up and the whole affair was quickly forgotten.

The veterinary costs of large animals like horses can be enormous, particularly when you have twenty. With different histories and ages, and varying levels of health. As with all the animals we attempted to keep costs down by trying to make sure as far as possible that the animals were at ease in the sanctuary. The herd animals such as the goats, sheep, donkeys and horses were given as much freedom as possible and allowed to sort out their own hierarchy and pecking orders. We resisted the lectures by our vets to spend fortunes on vaccinations, chemical wormers and other expensive drugs. One day when Patrick, our huge Clydesdale, went lame and could hardly walk, our vet diagnosed an abscess in his front foot. We knew from Patrick's record card that he had suffered an abscess in a rear foot only a month or so before Sue and I took over the management of the sanctuary. The previous manager had called in a vet who recommended anaesthetising Patrick so that the abscess could be dealt with by surgery. However, the record card also showed that Patrick had in fact 'died' under the anaesthetic and emergency action had to be taken to save him.

We told our vet that we didn't want to risk losing Patrick for an abscess and he agreed instead to try an old country method of drawing out the abscess with a bran poultice. We made a sock out of a sack, filled it with hot bran three times a day, and inserted Patrick's dinner-plate sized foot. Sue also put him on a dosage of fifty garlic pills a day to combat infection. After four days Patrick was fully recovered.

Of course there are limits to herbal remedies, flower remedies and spiritual healing – just as there are to conventional veterinary medicine. One of our favourite ponies was Red, who having lost his home came to us at the comparatively young age of twenty. He was a bit of a loner and took a long time to really settle into the herd, but eventually ended up quite high in the pecking order. He had been with us three years when we noticed a slight discharge from one nostril. It rapidly worsened and smelled terrible. Our vets considered that a tumour might be the cause of the problem and suggested we should seek an appointment with Langford Veterinary Hospital to examine him. We took him up to Bristol in a hired trailer, with Sue and I taking it in turns to be with him in the back in case he found it stressful. He travelled well and was received with great compassion by the vets and students at Langford, but the news was bad. Our vet's diagnosis was correct – a malignant tumour that was growing fast and which was inoperable. However, opinion was unanimous that he was not in any pain and it was agreed we should take him back to Ferne and keep him closely monitored.

The weeks rolled on and although Red never exhibited any signs of distress, the swelling became very large and the discharge so heavy and foul-smelling that we decided to have him euthanised before he became depressed and miserable. Our vet put him down with an intravenous injection while he munched some pony nuts from a bucket.

My own personal joy at taking horses and donkeys into the sanctuary was from the knowledge that whatever had happened to them in the past, none of them would ever have to carry or pull a human being again. Whether they lived another two years or twenty they would be free to do whatever they liked in the company of their own kind. They were no longer the servants of man – on the contrary, from now on we were their servants.

I can remember most of them as individuals as I write these words fifteen years after I left Ferne. 'Smithy', a 29-year-old bay gelding who had lost his winter grazing and stabling and who had been well-cared for during his life. 'Blue', a race-horse who never quite made the grade due to repeated lameness, but who unusually had an owner who gave Blue retirement in a sanctuary rather sending him for slaughter to end up in a can of dog food. As recent scandals have shown, many race horses, even those with household names, have been found dumped, depressed and starving in remote fields well away from the public's gaze.

Race horses are very delicate and winters were always a problem for Blue. He really should have been stabled during the cold weather, but this would have meant isolating him from the herd. So he had to wear a coat which had to be monitored constantly as somehow he always managed to have it hanging half on and half off.

There was tiny Donald, a 20 year old New Forest cross pony of only twelve and a half hands, taken from his owners by the RSPCA because they insisted on allowing overweight people to ride him when he was clearly not strong enough. Cindy was another favourite – so gentle, but always overweight and initially so arthritic that if she lay down she couldn't rise unaided. Three months on Dene's Greenleaf tablets cured that problem.

Beadle was a huge Shire horse with a dappled coat that positively glistened in the summer. He had come to Ferne before us, his record revealing that he had been abused by his owner who beat him around the head with a stick for the slightest mistake in his life of slavery. For the rest of his life Beadle remained 'head-shy' and would physically wince and shut his eyes at any sudden hand movement.

Lucky was a handsome 16 hands high strawberry roan, serving as a member of Her Majesty's Royal Navy at Yeovilton air station in Somerset. As well as ceremonial duties, 15-year-old Lucky was ridden by members of the station's saddle club. However, he kept going lame and eventually officers decided that his naval career should be ended. There are few horse enthusiasts willing to take on an animal which cannot be ridden and it looked for a while that Lucky was destined for the continental meat trade to which he was worth £200. Fortunately, gentle Lucky was highly popular with a group of female members of the saddle club and these 'wrens' offered to raise the £200 to 'buy him out' so that he could retire to Ferne. The navy eventually agreed and Lucky arrived at Ferne with a small delegation of his 'rescuers'. Free of saddles, bits and bridles, he never went lame again.

Lucky 'bought out' of the Navy by WRENs

Gregory was a hunter whose legs had been ruined by his idiotic owner who in his eagerness to be in at the kill galloped Gregory on hard roads too hard and too often. When the hounds are in full cry and the horn is blowing, many hunt riders get so carried away with the excitement and bloodlust of it all that they forget the old hunting adage; '*It 'aint the 'unting what 'urts the 'orse's 'ooves, it's the 'ammer, 'ammer, 'ammer on the 'ard 'igh road.*' Still, I suppose Gregory was lucky that his owner had enough of a conscience to allow him a peaceful retirement instead of having him shot and fed to the hounds – the fate of many a fox hunter's horse! Gregory was Patsy's first lieutenant throughout his life at Ferne and was never more than a few yards from her shoulder.

I shall always be grateful for the insight into the world of the horse that Ferne gave me. The mysterious dignity the equine species retains despite thousands of years of human exploitation can only be properly appreciated in a herd of horses freed from the straps, bits, leather and chains with which we have enslaved them.

Birds

Just as pigs are unfairly labelled as 'dirty', birds are regarded as unintelligent, 'bird-brained' creatures. In our experience birds of all species, domestic or wild are a lot more brainy than most folk think – and even display a lively sense of humour!

A Yeovil vet rang us to ask if we could take in a tame jackdaw that had been captured in a garden and brought into his surgery. We collected him, named him Rocky and offered him an empty bedroom that had a small French window opening out onto a narrow balcony. What a character! And what a menace! He would spend his days in the trees or on the roof waiting for someone to venture into the open. He would swoop down and land on human heads and proceed to pick ears, teeth and even noses with his sharp beak. It would have been bad enough if he had restricted these attacks to Ferne's staff, but even visitors were not safe.

During the drought of 1976 we had arranged for a mechanical digger to scoop out large pit in the paddock nearest the house. A lorry full of blue clay had been delivered and the idea was that once we had 'puddled' the clay into the pit, we would channel in a small nearby spring to provide us with a pond containing thousands of gallon of water. However, the spring was rapidly dwindling to a trickle and the clay was beginning to dry out. If it cracked it would not form a proper seal and the water would merely seep away in to the earth.

I had heard on the radio news that the drought was so intense that in some parts of the country, fire brigades were taking tenders of water around to remote communities and that some were even watering cricket pitches. Only a couple of weeks previously we had re-homed a dog with a local fire-chief and on the pretence of checking how the dog was progressing, I gave him a call. During the conversation I asked him whether there was any chance that we could have a delivery of water to fill our pond as our spring was drying up. He said that he didn't think he could help as there had been a lot of media and public criticism of various fire services for wasting water on cricket pitches and bowling greens. Then he had a thought. 'You've got a thatched roof on that farm-house haven't you?' he asked. I affirmed the fact. 'And you've got no mains water or a static water source either?' he added. I confirmed that the entire sanctuary was dependent on a well which was itself getting low. That was good enough for him. He said that he could justify filling our pond on the grounds that if there was a fire in our thatched roof it would not be possible to put out unless there was a large static water supply close by.

Two days later a huge water tender filled from the nearby river Yarty, arrived at Ferne. Our friendly fire chief, tall and dignified, was in full uniform giving instructions with an obvious air of authority. After three trips by the tender to and from the river, the pond was full and the fire-chief ordered the pumps to be switched off. Everything was suddenly silent as his men looked to their chief for the order to pack up the equipment. Before he could speak Rocky swooped out of the sky, landed on his cap and started trying to insert his sharp beak into the fire-chief's ears. The sudden aerial attack gave him quite a scare and he yelled and flung his arms around in panic trying to beat off the dive-bomber, his authority and dignity rapidly evaporating. After we rescued him and ex- plained to him that Rocky was a tame Jackdaw with a warped sense of humour, he saw the funny side of it and playfully warned his smirking crew not to repeat the story back at the station. From then on we tried to remember to warn all visitors about Rocky's games, but we had to make many more apologies.

Sue's mother came to stay for a few days. A real 'Eastender' from Walthamstow and very nervous of many of the creatures she found sharing our environment. We reassured her that they were all placid and none would do her any harm, but we forgot to tell her about Rocky!

At 6 am on the first morning of mum-in-law's visit, I awoke to a strange wailing sound. I strained my ears and tried to identify the plaintive cry. Was it a goat crying in the distance? Or was one of the sheep in trouble? I nudged Sue awake. I asked her what she thought it was. Sue sat up.

'It's in the house,' she exclaimed. We rose and crept out onto the landing. 'It's coming from Mum's room,' said Sue looking concerned. Sure enough, the eerie wail came again.

'Perhaps she's having a nightmare,' I ventured as Sue turned the door handle, opening the door a couple of inches. We both peered in through the crack and saw Sue's mother lying in bed, rigid with fear, white-knuckled fingers clutching the sheet over her lower face and nose, and with her eyes pinched tightly closed. And stood on her forehead was Rocky, the tip of his beak firmly gripping her eye-lashes as he tried to pull open her eye. 'Oh get off Rocky,' snapped Sue, rushing into the room and brushing the big bird off the bed.

He flapped to the open window and sat on the sill and 'yacked' at us while he tugged mischievously at the curtain cords and Sue's mother explained to us what had happened. She had awoken early. The window was open and she just lay there listening to the early morning summer sounds, when 'this big black bird' landed on the window ledge. 'I was fascinated,' she said. 'Suddenly it hopped into the room and sat on the end of the bed just peering at me. I was amazed, I've never seen a wild bird that close and I thought it didn't realise I was there.' Then, with the horror still audible in her voice, she explained how the bird had hopped sideways up the bed towards her. 'I just froze and I tried to pull the sheet over my face, but it jumped onto the pillow and looked me straight in the eye. I closed my eyes tight and it started to tug at my eye-lashes with its beak. That's when I began to yell,' she continued. 'I daren't do anything except try to call for help out of the corner of my mouth.'

It was this stifled wail that had awakened me. Poor mother-in-law. What a shocking experience! We laughed for days.

Chickens are generally thought to be pretty stupid. The way we keep millions of them, I suppose it would trouble too many consciences if we thought they were anything other than stupid. But hens are far from unintelligent, as anyone who has given a half-decent life to one can confirm. Sue and I were returning to the sanctuary in the van one day, having visited another animal rescue centre in South Dorset. It was early evening and already dark when we swept round a bend on a village and I just managed to swerve around some dark object in the road. I brought the van to a halt and Sue leapt out and ran back. Seconds later she was clambering back into the front seat with something clutched to her chest. 'Get going,' she ordered. 'What is it?' I asked. 'A chicken,' she replied as we sped away.

That was how 'Exide' the battery-hen came to Ferne. We had in fact been driving past a 'poultry processing plant' (which sounds better than 'slaughter-house') and Exide must have fallen off a lorry or escaped from the plant while she and thousands more were being transferred from cage to conveyor line for 'processing'. She was a typical example of a hen that has spent twelve months in a battery cage; large bald patches and with her few feathers worn, soiled, bent and broken. Her claws were overgrown from twelve months of standing on wire mesh and she had been drastically de-beaked. How can there be any doubt that birds kept in battery cages suffer cruelty when they end up in such a terrible condition?

Exide was lucky. Somehow she had avoided being hung by the feet upside down on a conveyor belt. According to reports of the Government's own advisory body, the Farm Animal Welfare Council, she would have had a fair chance of missing the electric stunning machine, and of being dragged conscious into scalding water used to soften the few feathers such birds have left. She had also managed to avoid having her feet and legs broken when dragged from her cage and crammed with others into more cages for transportation. And unlike many of her kind she also managed to avoid dying of exposure being transported in freezing conditions from the farm (if you can describe such factories as 'farms') to the 'processing plant' (if you can describe such brutality as 'processing').

Technically she was not ours, but 'finders were keepers' in our book that night.

Exide showed her appreciation for the rescue by laying an egg in Sue's lap as we drove through the night back to Ferne. After a few weeks of careful rehabilitation she was scratching around the yard with our ever-growing flock of bantams and ducks. She was a very bright bird and quickly learned that by following the pigs around as they rooted in the paddock, she would get plenty of

'Exide' presented us with an egg

worms and grubs. She learned the same about human beings who carried spades or garden forks!

It was Exide that provided one of the most hilarious incidents in my entire seven years at Ferne. We had several huge and very overweight Muscovy ducks and drakes. These greedy birds never flew. Their scrounging for food was only interrupted for the occasionally waddle to the pond for a drink and a paddle. Despite

'Exide' fully feathered with bantam friend 'Dove'

their size and ungainliness the drakes were very randy, and like so many male birds, far from gentle suitors. Their technique was crude but effective. They would suddenly rush at a female, grab a wing or neck in their beak and clamber on the unfortunate female's back, squashing her flat. The actual 'act' would be over in seconds, after which the drake would slide off exhausted while the female rushed away squawking to join the other females amongst whom there would be much sympathetic tail-wagging, head-bobbing and hissing – as she recounted her awful experience.

A Muscovy drake's penis when aroused looks like a foot-long, thin, white corkscrew. When he has got his breath back he too lumbers off, dragging his limp, open-coiled penis behind him. I watched the whole shocking scene from the kitchen window one day and saw the big drake, his latest conquest over, waddle past Exide as she scratched around in the dust of the yard. Suddenly, out of the corner of her eye she espied the great succulent white worm moving past. She pounced and gave it a mighty whack with her beak. The Muscovy drake quacked in pain and tried to waddle faster, falling over his own feet and beating his huge useless wings as Exide ran along behind after the speeding worm and giving it further blows in an effort to slow it down.

Eventually, crying with laughter, I had to intervene and rescue the distraught drake by picking him up and putting him over a wall out of the sight of Exide.

The drake suffered no permanent injury, but from then on he was a lot more careful about where he ambushed his females – particularly as many more rescued battery hens were later to join Exide at the sanctuary.

As yet it is not fashionable or profitable to keep ducks in cages. In that they are at least luckier than parrots, budgerigars and canaries. I just cannot understand why cage-birds are so popular. Is there anything more depressing than looking at a little bird deprived of its evolutionary birthright of flight staring out at the world through the bars of a cage.

One canary we took in had never been out of its foot-square cage in twelve years! And his owners hadn't even bothered to give him a name. When he arrived, not only couldn't he fly, but he could hardly even walk, owing to a long-neglected wasted foot.

Our first task was to massage his foot each day with Bach Rescue Remedy cream to try and get some life and movement into it. After a few weeks, Pickwick, as we named him, could walk better and was beginning to use his foot to grip his perch. Each day we carried his cage out into the fresh air for an hour or two, and finally, he went into a small aviary which he shared for a while with six blind guinea-pigs! After a week or so he could splash around in a bird-bath and climb onto a low perch to groom himself.

Pickwick sang gloriously; his clear tune plainly heard above the songs of the wild birds in the garden. Every day, we took him out and launched him gently into the air so that he could learn to use his wings and his tail feathers. His flights got longer and longer before he would run out of puff and land rather clumsily, but safely, in the long grass. He always had to be launched as he never seemed to have the confidence to actually leap into flight off my hand. Neither would he use his tail to change direction or brake, but always flew dead straight up through the garden.

We persevered and I was determined to keep working on him until he actually learned to spring with his own power into his ever-improving flight. I had an idea in my head that before he came to end of his life, Pickwick would learn to fly unaided so that we could build him a big aviary where he could fly and sing to his heart's content.

Then at last it happened. I was walking out into the garden with him on my hand one beautiful sunny morning. Suddenly he took off without being launched, flew strongly for ten yards, turned sharply to the left, and as my breath froze in my throat, he flew straight into a stone wall. He was dead before he hit the ground. I was stunned by the tragedy, and too choked up with guilt to talk about to anyone about it for days. But at least he flew, and upon reflection I was pleased that Ferne gave him the chance to experience flight after his 12 years incarceration in a cage. However, Pickwick's last flight was not the only occasion that a bird took to the air in heart-stopping circumstances!

One of our ambitions at Ferne was to build a Wildlife Rescue Unit and as staff numbers increased we were able to release Gary from the kennels to concentrate on his main interest – wildlife. He was already an excellent wildlife photographer and when not working with the dogs spent much of his free time wandering the surrounding countryside in search of subjects. Once given the task of building wildlife facilities however, the camera was put away and with his partner Helen and any other volunteers he could gather, Gary worked long hours erecting aviaries and pens for injured birds. He begged and borrowed equipment for a small hospital room and was soon caring for his first patients.

A crow had been found wandering in the road, having evidently been hit by a vehicle. We could not detect any injuries but the bird was totally blind. Gary decided that as the bird showed no sign of panic when handled and happily consented to hand-feeding, the best course was to keep the bird in a hospital cage for a few weeks to see if its sight returned. Sometimes blindness caused by an impact can be temporary.

The crow settled well and after a few days was quite happy to sit on Gary's arm while he wandered round the sanctuary. However, one day, the crow suddenly took off without warning and flapping powerfully flew high into the branches of one the large ash trees, clamped its strong claws onto a branch and hung on.

And there it stayed, fifty feet up the tree, while Gary sent Helen running for a ladder. Poor Helen returned dragging a heavy ladder and desperately trying to fight her way through a dozen goats all trying to get out through the gate as she was trying to come in with the ladder. Gary, his eyes glued on the crow in case it moved, was oblivious to Helen's game battle with a ladder, a heavy gate and a dozen awkward goats. 'Come on Helen, what are you doing?' he yelled over his shoulder impatiently.

Red-faced and breathless with the effort, Helen dragged the ladder towards the tree where Gary lifted one end and pushed it up the trunk. 'Up you go then Helen!' said Gary chivalrously. Helen pouted and considered protesting, but thought better of it and wearily mounted the ladder. Even on the top rung she was still twenty feet below the crow and too low to climb into the large limbs of the ash. Gary ran and fetched a long rigid length of plastic tubing and handed up to Helen as she balanced precariously at the top of the ladder. Gary urged her to try and topple the crow from its perch. 'It'll probably land in the field,' he suggested.

Helen waved the black tubing, but it was still far short of the crow's perch. Then, for some reason, the bird took off again and flew strongly out over the paddock fence heading north. In panic Gary set off in pursuit, stumbling across the paddock, not daring take his eyes of the flying bird. The first obstacle was the six feet high chain-link fence of the paddock. With his eyes still glued on the strongly flying crow Gary climbed the fence, missed his footing at the top and fell splat into the muddy ditch the other side.

Scrambling to his feet, he lost sight of the bird – then spied it again turning west. Gary set off again, his pullover heavy with mud and his Wellington boots picking up more with every stride. The bird flew on down towards the valley, clearing the spinney while Gary chased on behind ever more desperately. The bird was off the sanctuary air-space now and flying over Vernon Larcombe's farm. With lungs bursting Gary kept running, driven on by pure compassion and concern for the sightless bird. Down Vernon Larcombe's track he ran, through the farm yard with farm collies snapping at his heels, and chickens scattering in panic. Gary floundered on, chin jutting forward with determination and eyes straining aloft at the rapidly disappearing crow that flapped majestically onward in the direction of the coast. Then it was almost gone – just a speck in the distance, as Gary collapsed with his arms hanging over a farm gate, gasping for breath and too upset to furnish the baffled Larcombe family with an explanation.

Gary trudged home – disconsolate, dejected, mud-splattered,

dripping with sweat. And there he found us, suppressing our laughter as the blind crow sat contentedly on Helen's arm. Gary had been chasing a perfectly fit and healthy crow halfway across Devon while his blind bird had already landed in the field next to the paddock. When Gary had fallen off the fence and was extricating himself from the mud, he had missed seeing the crow land. Back on his feet he had spied another crow coincidentally flying over. And that was the bird he had been pursuing.

Another crow which caused a great deal of laughter was Korky. He came to us already tame, having been found as a fledgling and hand reared. His owners had to part with him following complaints about him landing on heads and scaring the life out of neighbours over-influenced by Alfred Hitchcock's *The Birds*. Their only other choice was to cage him and fortunately for Korky they rejected the idea as unacceptable. So he came to Ferne where birds landing on heads were nothing unusual.

What a devil Korky was. His greatest delight was sneaking up behind one of the yard dogs dozing in the yard and giving it a painful tweak with his powerful beak. The enraged dog would yelp and turn to attack the assailant, whereupon Korky would lift off the ground with one flap of his wings and glide a yard or two away. He would then shout obscenities at the growling dog, head stretched forward, bobbing up and down with each raucous '*caw*'. As soon as the dog walked away, Korky would dance sideways along behind, and dart in again to grab and twist another hank of hair, only to glide away again to taunt his chosen victim. There is no doubt whatsoever that this torment was inflicted for pure entertainment and is an illustration that birds have plenty of in-telligence. The dogs hated him, but they quickly learned that he was far too crafty to be caught.

At night Korky slept in a spare room, coming and going as he pleased through an open window. Early each morning he would pound on the bedroom door or peck chunks of plaster out of the wall until someone got up and filled a sink with water for his morning bath and splash.

One day he simply disappeared. He had been spending more time flying around the sanctuary, calling to other crows from the tops of our huge Beech trees. But he had always returned to his room at night to roost. One night he didn't come in and there was an eerie silence in the morning instead of the usual hammering on the door. We never saw him again and can only hope that he found himself a mate and had the sense not to tweak the tails of dogs in the presence of shotgun-toting farmers!

Unfortunately there is a great deal of bigoted and ignorant persecution of crows and their cousins the harmless rook, the lively jackdaw, the chattering magpie and the spectacular jay. They are amongst the most intelligent and fascinating of Britain's wild creatures – still likely to be seen hanging on the gibbet-line of gamekeepers – the lackeys of wealthy landowners whose idea of conservation is the factory farming and slaughter of millions of foreign pheasants.

A less demanding Ferne resident was Sybil the swallow, later renamed Chad. He came in as a barely fledged chick that had been found in a Chard garden. Right from the start he yelled loudly to be fed and happily tucked into tiny bits of raw meat dipped in egg yolk. He became very tame and was soon flying around the yard. The problem was that he seemed to have no idea about catching his own food even though there were plenty of other swallows around from whom he could have learned by example. When Chad was hungry he would just fly down and land on one of us, and yell to be fed, fluttering his little wings.

We fed him maggots and caught him flies. By teasing him with dead flies we eventually tempted him to snatch them from our fingers, but while he joined the other swallows sitting on our telephone cables he still wouldn't catch his own insects. He insisted on landing on a shoulder, peering into one's eyes and yelling for food. A Harlech Television outside broadcast crew came one day to make a short diary film about the sanctuary. When filming was over, the three-man crew spent more than an hour wandering round the yard, swatting flies and feeding them to Chad who sat on the hay cart surveying the scene with great interest while steadily becoming more and more bloated.

We soon learned that his apparent inability to catch his own food was just bluff! One day he suddenly joined in with the other swallows swooping over the pond catching insects and after feeding sat with them chattering and gossiping on the telephone cables.

He stopped flying to us and was soon indistinguishable from the rest of the flock. In the autumn Chad and all the swallows left for their amazing and perilous flight south. The following summer we watched out for their return and wondered whether Chad was amongst them, and whether he would make himself known to us. One swallow did land on the bedroom window sill and peer in, but flew away when we moved towards him. Was it Chad? We like to think so.

Another little soul that made a real impression on us was Delta, a young swift found grounded with a damaged wing at a local garage. He was a very cheerful and plucky little chap who was content to sit on a log in the surgery while his wing gradually healed, eating tiny pieces of meat from our fingers. When his wing had healed we began the difficult task of getting him back into the air. Once young swifts leave their nest, they eat, sleep and even mate on the wing. Their long wings and stubby little legs make it impossible for them to take off from the ground like other birds. If they find themselves grounded their only hope of taking flight is to scrabble along the ground to the base of a tree or post and climb up high enough to drop off into flight. If a swift is found on the ground and appears to be strong and uninjured, find a nearby open grassy space and try throwing it into the air. You will probably find that it quickly soars away high into the sky.

If Delta was to be restored permanently to the skies, his wing muscles would need re-building to the peak of fitness. We took him out into the fields each day and launched him. At first he could only fly a few yards before dropping into the grass, but after six weeks he could climb to forty or fifty feet and fly two hundreds yards. Several times he flew so far that he landed out of sight and we had to conduct painstaking searches for him. It became too risky to continue in this manner and we were faced with the dilemma that he was too strong to benefit from flying in an aviary, but not strong enough to release and migrate thousands of miles to Africa. After hours on the telephone we negotiated a free trip south for him with South African Airways and through a journalist friend placed Delta's story in several South African newspapers. This resulted in more than 300 volunteers in Africa willing to meet him off the plane, feed him up for a few days and release him.

Sue preparing Delta for take-off

As the day of his departure approached we continued Delta's flying sorties in the cattery garden (with the cats all shut away!). He became noticeably agitated (which we put down to sensing the approaching migrating season) but we also noticed that his flying became a little weaker. We observed him closely and there was no doubt that his broken wing had healed with a tiny degree of mis-alignment. This would not have mattered much to a blackbird or a pigeon, but swifts are the fastest and most skilful fliers in the world

116

and their equipment has to be perfect. We decided that it would be wrong to send Delta to South Africa unless we were sure that he could fly as well as any other swift. So we called off the whole exercise and scoured Britain for some sort of tropical aviary where he could spend the winter and where we could re-assess his flying abilities the next Spring. We found the ideal place in Gloucestershire that had another swift with a similar problem, but the day before we were due to deliver Delta, and after his daily 'cattery' flight, he settled onto his log, closed his eyes and died.

The little bird's spirit and fortitude, and his trusting nature touched all the Ferne staff. We had cared for him for eight weeks (the local RSPCA wildlife centre told us they had never managed to keep one alive for more than two weeks) and we had seen him soaring in the sky and hand-fed him several times a day. It was such a shame that he was never fully restored to the wild, but anyone involved in wildlife rescue will confirm that such heartbreak is common when dealing with sensitive and delicate wild birds.

Wild Animals

As we built up the sanctuary during the mid 1970s we always intended to make a major commitment to wildlife rescue and rehabilitation. Once the cattery, new kennels and stables had been completed and Gary and his girl-friend Helen appeared to be settled at Ferne, we began to plan a full-scale wildlife rescue service. But even before then we had been taking in orphaned and injured foxes, mostly cubs. The first to arrive was Vicky, a cub whose mother had been killed by poison – still illegally used by some game-keepers. Her rescuer was successfully hand-rearing the cub, but she decided to pass him onto us after a local bloodsports supporter had approached her and offered to buy the cub 'for the Hunt'.

Vicky was already very tame, but lonely. We gave her the company of a little mongrel puppy named Princess and they played and enjoyed mock-battles for hours. As they got older Princess came out of their pen to play with the other dogs around the yard, but Vicky rarely ventured out through the open-gate. Occasionally she would leave the security of the pen, but would either panic and scamper back in, or find a quiet spot to curl up asleep until we picked her up and returned her to the pen. She had little of the boldness inherent in many cubs. For instance we hit on the idea of picking up dead animals such as rabbits and squirrels killed on the local roads. We thought that this would teach Vicky to identify natural prey, but when we put the first dead squirrel into her pen, she was terrified of it. It was some time before she grasped the idea that such things could be eaten.

We lived in hope that Vicky might go back to the wild and live in the comparative safety of the sanctuary boundaries. But out hopes were dashed when at eight months old she started having fits. She

Vicky was our first fox

would throw herself around the floor in a frighteningly volatile fashion and although the fits only lasted a minute or so, she was always totally exhausted afterwards. We put her on regular doses of skull-cap and valerian herbal remedies for nervous conditions; this certainly reduced both the intensity and frequency of the fits.

It was obvious that Vicky could never be rehabilitated back into the wild, but we designed her a lifestyle to include as much pleasure as possible – plenty of attention, games with compatible dogs, a comfortable bed and good food. She would have a mild fit every month or so and quickly recover; until after two years at Ferne, Vicky suddenly went into a fit one day and had another three over the next forty-eight hours. The last one was very distressing to watch – she appeared to be conscious and terrified of something attacking her from the right hand side. There was nothing we could do until she wore herself out. We kept her subdued until the vet arrived and he felt that she must have been suffering from a brain lesion from which the chances of recovery were very slight. So while she lay resting, our vet deftly slipped a needle into her vein and she passed peacefully away.

By then we had three other foxes – all male. Rufus, Foxy and Merlin. Merlin was a real handful. Raised in an RSPCA dogs' home he thought and acted as a dog. He would roll on his back to have his stomach rubbed, wag his tail from side to side whenever he saw a dog, and scream with excitement if anyone spoke to him. All three foxes lived in the wired-in cattery garden and had dug their own entrance to an underground 'earth' beneath the cattery bungalow. They went under in the morning to spend the day asleep and the cats enjoyed the garden in peace. In the evening the foxes would emerge and be fed amongst great squealing and mock battles. They would also leave some of their food uneaten and dash off to a far corner of the garden to dig a hole in which to cache the surplus food.

Foxy and Rufus had a very healthy respect for the cats – as do all wild foxes. The stories about foxes killing cats are almost always nonsense; foxes are far too intelligent to risk an eye in a confrontation with a spitting ball of fury and claws – particularly when they can survive by scavenging on virtually any type of food. I've even known foxes dig up the remains of dead animals eighteen months after burial. They will eat rats, mice, voles, fruit, earthworms and beetles, raid bird-tables and thrive in almost any terrestrial habitat on the planet. Why would such an animal risk all by taking on a cat? I spent many hours watching the inter-reaction between the foxes and the cats in the cattery garden. The cats were always 'top-dog' – if you know what I mean! I even witnessed eight-week old kittens drive fully-grown Rufus off his food and steal it. Of course foxes have been seen carrying dead cats and moggy remains have been found at fox earths. But there is no doubt that the foxes have merely scavenged dead cats killed by that most ruthless predator of both foxes and cats – the motor car.

That said, Merlin was an exception. Regarding himself as more domestic dog than wild fox, he started stalking the cats and pouncing on them for fun. When a cat spat at him, back arched and coat bristling, Merlin would back off a yard, crouch, wag his tail, wait until the cat turned away and then pounce again. Once he even bit a cat and so until we could build our planned fox pen we had to change the system. We shut the foxes in their den under the cattery bungalow during the day, and at night shut the cats into their bungalow while the foxes prowled the garden.

We thought this arrangement would last for a while until we could design and build a proper fox compound. But Merlin soon forced us to speed up our plans. Early one morning, I went into the yard-dogs' room to open the double-doors out into the yard. This was always a moment of great excitement for the dozen or so 'yardies' who were regarded as permanent residents and unlikely candidates for re-homing. Once the doors were thrown open they would all rush out as a pack and tear around the yard and orchard barking to greet the new day. I was just pinning the doors back when I heard the barks turn to yelps and the entire pack came tearing back through the doors into their night-quarters – followed, hot on their heels, by a grinning and exuberant Merlin – the first case in history of a fox chasing a pack of dogs.

The dogs were terrified of him and I had to shut them in and call for help to try and catch Merlin. I expected to find at least a couple of dead bantams around as Merlin had almost certainly been out before daylight, but they had wisely stayed high on their perches and all the chickens and ducks were still safely shut in their night-sheds. From then until we built our new fox pen, Merlin roamed the sanctuary free at night, and early each morning we would catch him and shut him in for the day.

Soon the three foxes were joined by Basil, who having been injured in a road accident, had lived ever since at a west country wildlife park which later collapsed with financial problems. After our 600-square-yard fox pen had been built, he and some of the foxes were quite content to stay in captivity. Its six feet high fencing had an overhang to prevent escape over the top and wire mesh laid along the ground for a couple of feet all round the inside of the fence to prevent digging out. We incorporated tunnels, bushes, long grass and various platforms on which some foxes would sun-bathe, doze or sit and watch the world go by. Other foxes hated the captivity and would pace the wire, or constantly attempt to climb the fence; if they didn't settle we let them go. We found that released foxes usually stayed within the sanctuary, returning each night for food. Gary fixed up a powerful lamp to observe the foxes at their food bowls and check whether they were well, but eventually they moved away to find their own territories and breed.

We had to accept that once off the sanctuary the foxes faced a world where the ignorant regarded them as 'vermin' to be shot, snared or dug out with dogs, where the callous sought their coats to sell to the disgusting fur trade, and where the bigoted saw them as sporting accessories to chase to exhaustion and death with dogs.

The story of Rufus illustrated the point. He had been brought in as the sole surviving cub after a gang of terrier-men had dug out the vixen and her cubs from an earth in Essex. The vixen was found dying, nailed to a tree while Rufus wandered lost and frightened nearby. He was rescued and came to Ferne where he grew into the perfect, classic, photogenic fox. Gary took scores of photographs of him – many used to this day on Christmas cards and calendars (and on the cover of this book!).

Eventually he dug out of his temporary pen behind the cattery and lived as a wild fox at night, but returned early each morning to spend the days curled up asleep in his pen. Later he decided to live free altogether, but would trot into the yard each night and sit on our kitchen doorstep until we called him into the kitchen for a lump of meat that he would grab and then dash off with it into the night.

We discovered that he was sleeping during the day behind the dog kennels. The dogs could not see him, but they could certainly smell him and in the early days would stand at the wire fence barking in his direction. Rufus was seemed oblivious to the clammer and the dogs soon gave up yelling at him. And so it went on for a couple of years, until one day the local Fox Hunt met nearby. The field next to the sanctuary was owned by the Master of the Hunt and contained an ancient and well-used badger sett. Hunted foxes often ran in our direction in an effort to find refuge in the sett, and our neighbour Vernon Larcombe, a tenant of the Master of the Hunt, was under orders to block-up the entrances of the sett when the Hunt was in the area.

Several times we were invaded by fox hounds causing mayhem amongst the animals. Indeed the very first week we were at Ferne hounds had to driven off with brooms after attacking a young orphaned roe deer being reared in a paddock at the sanctuary by the previous manager and his wife.

One afternoon the Hunt was in the field adjoining our south eastern boundary and I saw that a line of riders had been placed along our boundary hedge – presumably to turn back any fox and prevent hounds trespassing. The hounds were in full cry amongst the scrub and ferns; the Huntsman's horn furiously urging them on. We were fearful that the intended victim might be Rufus. The hounds hurtled through our neighbour's field, went quiet briefly as they lost the scent, and then erupted again as they re-found the fox's trail. The sounds disappeared and we thought they were gone, but within minutes they were heading back towards us. They hunted around the boundaries of the sanctuary for half and hour or so and then finally left us in peace.

We were reassured by the fact that we had not heard the Huntsman blow 'the kill' on his horn and we assumed that Rufus had been laid-up somewhere safe within Ferne while the hunters were nearby. But we were wrong. That evening we sat waiting for Rufus to come to the house for his usual snack. He appeared in the yard, but was clearly in trouble. He staggered weakly across the yard and collapsed on the kitchen step. I opened the door and gently picked him up in my arms. He seemed unconscious and I felt him die as I sat cradling him on the step.

Within three-quarters of an hour Rufus was on our vet's table for a post-mortem. No sign of poison, no bite-wounds or injuries, no worm-infestation or sign of disease. In fact, as our vet remarked, not meaning the irony; 'It's the healthiest animal I have ever had on this table.' He concluded that Rufus had simply succumbed to the exhaustion, terror and trauma of his encounter with the pack of forty hounds, and the bullies who follow them. I think I knew that day that before too long I would leave Ferne to spend my working life campaigning for a ban on hunting.

I've no doubt that the hunters went home after their day's charge around the countryside thinking to themselves; '*What a good day. Charlie gave us a great chase and got away to save his brush and run another day.*' But he hadn't. It is estimated that Fox Hunts in the United Kingdom kill around 20,000 foxes a year. The hunters claim in their propaganda that hunting with dogs is superior to other methods of killing, because 'the fox is either killed outright or gets away unscathed'. Not true. How many thousands of foxes escape at the cost of their constitutional health? How many crawl into an earth and never recover. Foxes are not like hares, deer, rabbits and other natural prey species. Throughout their evolution foxes have never been hunted long distances by other predators. No pack of wolves ever bothered chasing a small animal like a fox for mile after mile; the expenditure of energy in such a chase could not be recouped by the mouthful of meat each member of the wolf-pack could obtain at the end. Wolves hunt in packs to pull down large prey on which to gorge themselves. They rely on ambush and short chases of the weak and injured – not long exhausting pursuits of healthy animals.

The only way hunters can catch foxes with their hounds is to employ hunt servants to go out the night before the hunt and block-up all known fox earths, badger setts and drains, so that any fox found by the hounds the next day cannot use its natural defence from danger, i.e. diving down the nearest hole. And of course if a fox does find an unblocked hole during the hunt, the 'sportsmen' call for small terriers to be sent down either to drive out the fox or keep it under attack until it can be dug out and slaughtered by the brutal 'spade and terrier brigade' who can be found following every Hunt waiting for the opportunity to indulge their nasty natures.

We were all devastated by Rufus's pointless death. What had he ever done? His brothers and sisters had been killed by thugs who spiced up their own particular form of fox hunting by nailing his mother alive to a tree. He had survived that horror and had been reared to maturity at Ferne. He had taken the option of living free, while maintaining contact with the humans he trusted, only to be abused to death by other humans to whom he had never done any harm in his entire four years of life. And they wonder why some anti-hunt people break the law to stop hunters killing foxes!

We continued to take in rescued foxes and to rehabilitate those which were not too tame back to the wild. Mungo was seven years old when he came to Ferne having been rescued from pacing in circles in a tiny pen at a grim zoo in Essex where he had lived since being found as a cub with his tail torn out at the root. He found a much better life at Ferne and his disturbed behaviour soon ceased.

Tag and Charlie were two tiny cubs found wandering about on the A30 near Cricket St Thomas Wildlife Park. The finder of the two cubs took them into the Wildlife Park, who refused to take them in because they would grow up to be a threat to their pheasants being reared for shooting. Some 'wildlife park'! Scrap was another cub brought to Ferne from Dover in Kent. His rescuers cared for him deeply and even had him vaccinated against distemper and parvo-virus. However, they felt he needed the company of other foxes and the chance to go back to the wild.

All wildlife rescue centres receive plenty of foxes, particularly cubs in the Spring. Cubs are often assumed to be lost when seen wandering about unsupervised by an adult. Often they are not lost at all and if left alone will be collected later by their mother. However, it is wrong to assume that all lone cubs are only temporarily lost. Many vixens are killed on the roads and when their mother fails to return, the cubs get hungry and wander about in dangerous situations. If you see a cub on its own in a position of danger, for instance where dogs can get to it, or near accessible busy roads or if the cub is wet or cold, then it should be rescued. If the cub seems uninjured and healthy, offer it some tinned cat or dog food and keep it in until just after dark. Then place it in a quiet spot in a garden as near as possible to where it was found. Keep watch from a distance and hope that the mother finds her cub. If it's still alone a couple of hours later then assume it is genuinely in need of rescue, re-rescue it and call a reputable wildlife rescue organisation.

Fortunately badger cubs are much more rarely found lost or

Helen with fox cub Cleo and Grublin the badger

abandoned. We took one cub named Silver that had been rescued by Northampton Animal Rescue. She was a real charmer and followed Gary everywhere like a little dog and adopted a cupboard under the stairs in the hall as her 'sett' where she would sleep all day. She was extremely active at night and gave Gary many sleepless nights until the problem was solved by fitting a cat flap in the front door so she could spend the nights outside. She would be in and out several times each night and as often as not would be found snoring under Gary's bed in the morning. One morning there was no sign of her until almost by accident she was discovered curled up asleep in an old rabbit hole in the hedgerow bordering the main drive.

I was awakened one night by a horrendous screaming. I grabbed a dressing gown, pulled on my 'wellies' and ran out into the orchard with my torch. The screaming was coming from the other side of our boundary hedge and as I climbed over the bank in to our neighbour's field I saw a large sow badger giving Silver a real pasting. I shouted and ran towards the ferocious battle but it was not until I actually waded into the fight with my rubber boots that the big badger turned and hurtled off towards the sett on the nearby hillside. Silver scuttled off back towards the house, but instead of going through the cat flap, she dived beneath the rabbit hutches and refused to come out for more than 24 hours.

Clearly she had stumbled into the territory of the neighbouring family group and was attacked. When she did emerge from under the rabbit hutches she had quite nasty bites around the base of her spine (badgers tend to fight end to end) and to combat any infection we sprinkled the wounds with powdered rosemary a couple of times a day for a week or so. They healed well.

We believe that she was absorbed successfully into the colony eventually, because she was spotted a couple of times coming and going from the sett – seemingly without suffering further beatings. We saw less and less of her and hopefully her rehabilitation seemed to be completely successful.

A wild animal not native to Britain, but now spreading successfully through Britain's countryside, is the tiny Muntjac deer. Imported from Asia a hundred years ago as additions to zoos and parks, the Muntjac are now spreading through our woodlands and are so tiny that they can live in gardens for many months without the knowledge of the house-owners. Our first experience of handling one followed an accident in, of all places, West Drayton high street. No-one knew where the female deer appeared from, but having been hit by the car it staggered into some railings and was so dazed it was easily captured. A local vet found no broken bones, but recommended a few days rest to recover from its bruises and grazes.

Suitably tranquillised and hobbled the deer arrived at Ferne at midnight. We bedded her down in a stable and after a day or two she was eating well and seemed strong. However, we decided to keep her another week to make sure an injury to her foot had fully healed. The following week it was time for her to return to the wild, but where? At that time, the British Deer Society advised that Muntjac had not come as far west as Somerset. After a few phone calls we found a man who owned 500 acres in the Ashdown Forest and who did not permit any shooting or hunting on his land. He also had a wire pen in which he was willing to keep the deer for a few hours to recover from the journey before release into the forest. Muntjac are known to inhabit the Ashdown Forest and so the offer was too good to pass up.

First catch your deer! Although no bigger than a dog, Muntjac like all deer are extremely strong and athletic. It was my job to go into the stable to catch her and the only answer was a rugby tackle. This took some time while the deer was going round the stable like a 'wall-of-death' motorcycle. After a couple of bungled tackles

I managed to hold her down while a tranquilliser was administered. After a few minutes she had calmed down and was ready to be carried to the van, while I nursed my bruises and a thick-lip. Sue and I were accompanied by Fenella, taking it in turns to drive while the other two sat in the back with the deer which happily tucked into bananas, leaves and even our sandwiches. On the way we called into the local RSPCA wildlife centre to pick up a one-legged buzzard which was due to be released in the same part of Ashdown Forest.

Five hours later, just as it was getting dark, we arrived at a beautiful house deep in the forest. We carried her into the wire pen and advised the landowner to let her out in the morning when all traces of the tranquilliser would have cleared from her bloodstream. He later reported that when he approached the pen in the morning the deer took one look at him and burst straight through the wire and off into the forest!

Another casualty deer brought to Ferne was with us a lot longer. Guy was a Fallow deer fawn found at the roadside in the New Forest, apparently hit by a car and left for dead. He had suffered a brain haemorrhage which left him blind and paralysed, but the kind folk who found him were advised by their vet that the blindness and paralysis might only be temporary. The couple nursed him at their home until his eyesight returned and his little legs regained their use. Then they asked us to take him in for his final re-habilitation.

At first we put him in the goats' house and as his confidence grew we let him into the paddock with the goats which we assumed he would adopt as his new family. Not so! He took one look at Misty the Jersey cow and decided she was to be his new mother. They immediately became inseparable, although we had a few problems with the differing maternal practices between the two species. A deer will often leave her fawn hidden in undergrowth or long grass for lengthy periods and go off to browse a considerable distance away before returning to collect the youngster. The trouble was that Misty would return to the yard after a day out in the fields having forgotten to retrieve Guy. Misty seemed to expect Guy to be at home waiting for her and she would called mournfully until we had taken a couple of dogs out to find Guy's hiding place, where he would be contentedly chewing the cud waiting for Misty to return.

In fact it was Guy that had to change habits. After being left for one long stint too many, he learned to stay close to Misty wherever she went, and not to lie down where he could not keep her in constant view. While out with Misty, sometimes the herd of goats would be browsing nearby. Guy delighted in dancing in and around them and one or two goats would often join in the game and indulge in a little gentle sparring. He was rapidly growing into a strapping young Fallow buck. In March his antlers began to appear and we noticed that he was becoming much more independent of Misty, although she still doted on him and called anxiously if he was out of sight too long.

Then he suddenly left. It seemed he was around one moment and the next he was gone. It was Misty who alerted us to his departure. We noticed her standing staring over our boundary hedge and mournfully mooing. We went looking for Guy in the direction Misty was peering, but apart from a few tracks we could see no sign of him. Misty was upset for days, returning repeatedly to her spot by the hedge and calling for him, but we never saw or heard of him again. It was several days before Misty gave up calling and returned to her life with the goats, sheep and eventually the company of her own kind in Magpie, Queenie, and particularly our steer Muppet with whom she began a lifelong love-affair.

Of course virtually every cow in the country knows the pain suffered by Misty. They have to suffer it every year when they are robbed of their precious calves so that we humans can steal the milk. Anyone who lives in the countryside will know when the local herd of cows have lost their calves to the to the local livestock market or to the ports for export to some other country's satanic veal crate system – banned in the UK on grounds of cruelty. Often for several days and nights, those living near a dairy farm will hear the depressing constant lowing of the grieving cows calling their lost calves. At least Misty only went through the pain of losing her 'calf' once. I wonder why it is that we humans are the only animals in the world which not only drink milk beyond infancy and all through our lives, but also take it from the udders of a species not remotely like us?

Misty with her 'calf' Guy

Returning to our work for wildlife, once the local papers had published a few stories about the wild creatures Ferne had helped, we began to receive calls from people requesting emergency assistance. The landlady of a local pub on the banks of the river Yarty rang to ask if we could capture a lone swan hanging around the car park and barring the entrance to the bar with much hissing and wing-flapping. When Sue, Gary and a visiting friend arrived on the scene, there was a crowd of local yokels waiting to watch the fun. It was a real hunting pub adorned with the heads of foxes, badgers and even otters killed long ago by the pub's past clientele.

Our reputation of detesting bloodsports was well known in the area and both Sue and Gary were concerned that if the capture of the swan was bodged we would suffer much ridicule. Fortunately, the operation went perfectly and within minutes the swan was literally 'in the bag' and on its way to the Axmouth estuary. Also in the van was a Ferne Animal Sanctuary AA sign which had been stolen on our 'open day' earlier that Summer. Sue had spotted it at the pub where no doubt it was regarded every bit as much a trophy as the assortment of dead animals' heads inside.

We decided that we should get ourselves better equipped if we were going to become a local wildlife emergency call-out service. We needed cages, graspers, gloves, masks and all sorts of attire. I also felt it would be wise to obtain a humane-killer and fortunately a friend at the RSPCA arranged for me to be trained in the use of a captive-bolt gun and .32 pistol which the society agreed I could have on a long-term loan.

Apart from extensive practice on telephone directories, I only had to use a gun twice – once to kill a badger which had been run over twice and which was in a lot of pain, and the second time to kill a roe deer fawn which Boy Scouts had found pinned under a fallen tree. They brought it to Ferne and we called out a vet who was a deer expert. He concluded that it had a fracture of the spine and we expected him to recommend immediate destruction. However, he surprised us by suggesting that although the fawn was unlikely to recover to a level of fitness necessary for life in the wild, it might heal well enough for the animal to be offered a life with our goats in the sanctuary. He instructed us to ensure that the deer would need constant attention and would need gently turning every two hours to prevent fluid accumulating in its lungs.

All went very well for a couple of weeks. The fawn seemed very content in our hospital unit on soft deep bedding, enjoyed a really good appetite and was never alone for more than a few minutes. Then sadly something went wrong. One of the staff came rushing to the office to tell me that the deer had suddenly started screaming. I rushed to the hospital unit and the fawn was in a terrible state. If you've ever heard a deer screaming in pain or terror, you will never forget it. Gary was trying to soothe the animal and it seemed to settle a little. We decided to get the animal to the nearest veterinary surgery only six miles away, but as we gingerly carried it out of the unit, it began to scream again and the distressed staff urged me to put the deer out of its misery.

I can tell you that placing a gun-barrel on to the head of a deer and looking it in the eyes is the worst thing I have ever had to do. It's like shooting Bambi – even though you know that it is the only thing to do to relieve its pain. Fortunately the deer died instantly with the one shot, but I had to go off into a far field with the horses for an hour for a few private tears. The rest of the staff found their own quiet spots to do the same.

After that incident I found it even more difficult to understand how people can pick up a gun, point it at a beautiful and harmless creature such as a deer, and fire a bullet into it for pleasure! Over my eight years I was responsible for taking more than one hundred decisions to kill animals – never for any other purpose than to relieve suffering. Several times it was my own hand which carried out the deed. I always found it an awesome, painful and un-forgettable task. I can understand the satisfaction felt by someone like a professional veterinarian or deer stalker, when they carry out the job efficiently and humanely, but how anyone can get pleasure from shooting animals or birds is completely beyond my comprehension.

Gary continued to develop the wildlife unit and persuaded the Nature Conservancy Council (now English Nature) that our new aviaries and hospital, together with his expertise were well worthy of a licence to take in and rehabilitate birds of prey. Thereafter he and Helen managed to repair and restore scores of injured owls, buzzards and other raptors to the wild.

The strangest wild animal I actually dealt with myself was a crab. I was driving back to the sanctuary from Chard one hot summer's day when I saw something strange towards the edge of the road ahead. As I went past, I thought to myself; 'That looks like a crab! It can't be, we're at least twelve or fifteen miles from the nearest sea water.' But I was right. When I turned round and drove back, it was a crab; sitting in the road in the hot sun with frothy bubbles streaming from it mouth and having shed one of its claws. I drove like a maniac to Lyme Regis, but it died before I could return it to the ocean.

Animal Rescue

Most of our rescues were more successful – particularly when saving domestic animals. We were called out to a house where a dog and a kitten had been shut in and no tenant had been seen for seven days. The police were reluctant to come and help us break in, and we were just about to smash a window when a neighbour told us that the landlord of the property was the owner of a local factory. He was quickly located and he agreed to open up for us.

We were greeted by an appalling smell and a little terrier mongrel which dashed past us and thrust its head down a drain trying to reach the water. Someone brought out a bowl of clean water and he drank frantically, but otherwise seemed in reasonable condition. He had managed to get a cupboard open and had eaten a bag of sugar, but the kitten had not fared so well and was starving. We reported the situation to the police in the hope that they might liaise with the RSPCA and try to launch a prosecution, but we heard nothing more. Within weeks Scrumpy the dog and the Cherry the kitten were fit and well and settled into new caring homes.

We also went through a period when we were called out several times to rescue cats and kittens from rubbish tips – once having to persuade the workmen to stop using their bull-bulldozers while we set cage traps to capture a litter of very wild kittens.

A local animal feed manufacturer also called us out to trap a colony of feral cats living in the mill. The mill owners had been happy to have them there to keep down the rats and mice, but the local health authority insisted on the rodents being poisoned and the cats being removed.

I must admit that on one or two occasions our rescues sailed rather close to the wind – legally. Some people on a housing estate in a nearby town called and asked us to rescue a cat and kitten which a couple kept locked in a coal shed. Neighbours had complained to the local RSPCA Inspector without success.

The couple who owned the cats apparently went down the pub every night and came home very late and very drunk. A neighbour agreed to ring us as soon as the couple went out, but they warned us that the immediate neighbours who shared the couple's drive were very 'neighbourhood watch' and would undoubtedly ring the police if they saw someone sneaking about. The call came to inform us that the couple had departed to the pub and we drove to the estate – parking some way away from the house so as not to alert the next door neighbours to the arrival of a strange vehicle.

We sneaked down the drive in the dark with a couple of cat baskets. It was my job to open the shed door and get in without the cats escaping. It was a windowless shed and stupidly I had left my torch in the van. So I had to feel around in the pitch-dark for two cats which might well be terrified and wild, and try to get them into baskets! As it happened I had no trouble at all and quickly emerged covered in coal dust and cobwebs, but with the two animals safely in the baskets. We tip-toed up the drive, but as we glanced at the neighbour's house, we saw two people peering at us through the window. My mind raced as to how we could explain ourselves if they challenged us, but I needn't have worried. Four erect thumbs assured us that the neighbours totally approved of what we were doing. Back at the sanctuary the cats went onto our list of rescued 'strays' and were soon re-homed with caring families who remained unaware of the cats' true origins!

A dog rescued in similar circumstances was an eighteen-month-old lurcher bitch kept on a farm in Somerset, but which had spent her entire eighteen months of life chained to an old tea chest which served as a kennel. The farmer had apparently intended to train Petra (as we named her) as a sheep dog, but had never quite got round to it and she was never allowed off the chain.

Petra's rescuers knew when the owners were away from the farm. Petra was thin and extremely nervous, but not aggressive. She was attached to the chain by a piece of binder twine; instead of cutting it the rescuers rubbed it on the wall to make it look as if it had frayed and that she had simply escaped. We also relied on the fact that as often as not farmers will not report the loss of a dog for fear of discovering that during its freedom it had attacked someone's sheep and that they might be sued for thousands of pounds.

Once she had got used to us for a few days, we took her down to a deserted Dorset beach and let her off the lead – and immediately regretted it as she zoomed off along the beach like a rocket until she was just a dot in the distance. We were yelling our heads off and running in pursuit when we saw that the dot was getting bigger and in flash she was back past us and rapidly becoming a dot in the other direction. She was in a state of pure joy. For the first time in her life she could run as far and as fast as she liked. That first day she quickly tired and the next day she was too stiff to do more than hobble about. But daily visits to the beach enabled her to run all the long months of frustration out of her system. One day she actually ran up the almost vertical 100 feet high cliff face and scrabbled over the top out of sight. My heart was in my mouth as I thought of her running off into the countryside, but suddenly her grinning face appeared over the top, and she was half falling half running back down the cliff towards us. The last time I saw Petra she was lying fast asleep with her feet in the air on a settee in a caring home she shared with two other dogs and four cats.

I wonder how many other Petras there are chained up in farm yards around Britain. The television programme 'One Man and His Dog' paints an idyllic picture of the life of a working dog. My wife and I take walking holidays every year in places such as Cumbria, Yorkshire Moors, Peak District and North Wales. Many footpaths are routed through farms where often we tramp through yiked at by a pair of hysterical collies spinning at the end of rusty chains, or watched silently by a morose and muddy dog standing chained, cowed and shivering in an open barn. Worse, our passage through the farm may be monitored by the long rasping breaths from a whining dog's nose protruding from a gap under the door of a windowless shed. Of course not all farmers treat their animal servants with such contempt. Just too many of them!

In the dark early hours of one morning I answered a phone call purporting to be from 'the Animal Liberation Front'. The caller said that he had dozens of guinea pigs just rescued from the premises of a breeder who supplied animals for vivisection laboratories. The caller said that he would be arriving at Ferne within an hour and that he wanted to hand the rescued animals over to us. Great! It had only been a couple of years since I stood in the dock at Wilmslow Court facing seven years in prison for 'receiving and disposing of stolen goods' – namely two Beagles taken from the local ICI laboratories and dumped on Sue and me in the early hours. The Beagles had been used in smoking experiments which had been a major scandal exposed by the Sunday People newspaper who had managed to infiltrate ICI's staff. The police had been tipped off that we had the two dogs, but by the time they raided us we had already moved them on to safe houses. I admitted having the dogs but refused to reveal their whereabouts and was therefore charged with 'receiving and disposing stolen goods'. My defence was that it was an offence under the Protection of Animals Act and Abandonment of Animals Act for an owner or keeper of an animal to place it in a situation where it is likely to suffer.

As it turned out I was acquitted because the prosecution offered no evidence provided that I and my co-defendant, Michael Huskisson (who had been charged with stealing the dogs) agreed to be bound over to be of 'good behaviour' for two years. The two dogs were never recovered by ICI and both lived to a good old age in family homes. Incidentally, the crown was represented by Alex Carlile QC later to become a Liberal Democrat MP.

I considered that both Michael and I had been pretty lucky to avoid a lengthy trial, and I did not relish facing such a trauma again for 'receiving' stolen guineapigs! But, it was too late to think about it; they were on their way and we needed to arrange their reception.

An hour later we had erected two pens inside the hospital unit and we were sorting the sexes of more than 100 white albino guinea pigs. The two pens were identical sizes, but only five of the guinea pigs were female! They had travelled a long distance in boxes in the boot of a car and were very frightened.

Unfortunately the activists had not brought out some of the guinea pigs' food out with them and I told them that a change of diet, on top of the stress of the 'rescue' and transportation, could cause real problems.

Sure enough, after a few days, guinea pigs started to die. I called out one of our vets and he confirmed that the cause of death was digestive problems no doubt exacerbated by a drastic change of diet. He guessed the origin of the guinea pigs (the raid had been well reported in the media), but he said that his only concern was treating the animals. Despite his best efforts and our nursing we lost almost half of the little 'spooks' as we collectively named them. It was heartbreaking watching them suffer and die, one by one, over a period of a week or more.

Guinea pigs rescued from laboratory breeders

Meanwhile the media was reporting how the ALF 'liberators' paraded anonymously in black Balaclavas boasting how they had heroically saved these animals from vivisection. But ALF activists didn't have to hear the guinea pigs wheezing their last breaths or feel their dying convulsions – all because they didn't bother to take advice on the effects of stress and dietary changes in small nervous animals before they embarked on their 'rescue' mission.

Neighbours

To people who kill animals for fun, or who spend their lives rearing animals merely for their meat or skins, the concept of an animal sanctuary where animals are cared for by humans who have no intention of making a profit from them, is beyond their comprehension. I know local farmers had told people that it was outrageous that we were 'wasting' good farmland by allowing 'useless' animals to wander and feed upon it.

The very first week we were at Ferne, we were invaded by hounds of the Cotley Hunt. Following a second incursion a few weeks later, we used the local media to publicise our anger at the invasion and as a result received – a visit from the Hunt's Master, Colonel Eames. He arrived in the yard in his Landrover, swung his 'gammy' leg out of the vehicle and explained that he had come to make our acquaintance and apologise for his hounds trespassing on the sanctuary. 'It's a shame you bought this place,' he explained, 'because it's the fox's M1 through here.'

I tried to explain to him that the philosophy of the sanctuary and ourselves as individuals included a fundamental opposition to hunting and killing animals for human entertainment, but his condescending smile indicated that he didn't really understand. It was clearly beyond his imagination that someone could care so much about the pain of wild animals that we didn't even know, that we would not permit our land to be used for hunting. His final remarks while leaving, proved it beyond all doubt.

'Now that we've been introduced to each other, I'm sure we won't be having any more of these silly press stories if the odd hound should run across your field, will we?' he said – more as an instruction than a question.

'Colonel Eames, all I can say is that if one hound should as much as put its nose over our fence, I will firstly ring the press and then the sanctuary's lawyers,' I replied. It was obvious that people did not generally speak to the old Colonel in such terms, and he merely went a little red, smiled, and cheerfully wished us 'Good-day,' as he clambered back into his Landrover.

One day while out searching for a reported stray dog, I called at a farm less than a mile from us. The tenant farmer was very chatty and seemed quite interested in the purpose to which we were putting 'Downlands', the name by which he knew the property. The subject got around to fox hunting and he recounted how the previous week the Hunt's hounds had invaded his farm and stampeded his dairy cattle through an electric fence and into his crops. He said that one cow had tried to jump the fence and had spiked her udders on one of the metal fence posts. He had to call out the vet to treat the wound and administer antibiotics – which of course meant taking the cow out of milk production for ten days, and he spent the best part of the afternoon rounding up the agitated cattle and repairing the fence.

Unsurprisingly the experience had resulted in a drop in milk yield for a day or two. He smiled as he confided in me that the Hunt Master had called in to apologise him the evening of the incident and had pushed a five pound note into his top pocket as recompense for the ruined day and financial loss. And hunters wonder why rural public opinion against hunting almost matches that in the towns!

Colonel Eames was a polite and likeable old man who had hunted all his life. The Cotley pack has been owned by his family since the inception of the Hunt in the mid-nineteenth century. [*The Colonel died in 1987 and the Mastership passed to his son*]. Clearly we were far from welcome in the Hunt's territory, but even the Colonel himself condemned the tactics some of his Hunt supporters adopted in an effort to drive us out. I do not believe it to be an exaggeration to say that for almost five years we were subjected to a constant and vicious campaign of terrorism.

The large, white, wooden entrance gate and the sanctuary sign just inside, became the point of focus for the clash between the local bloodsports culture and Ferne's compassionate philosophy.

Firstly, the sign was blasted with shotgun pellets late one night. I called in the local press to photograph the damage and reported the incident to the police, but decided not to have the sign repaired so that visitors to the sanctuary could see for themselves the vandalistic nature of some of the local hunting mob. Then dead foxes and badgers began to adorn the main gate – apparently road-killed badgers and shot foxes. Next the main gate was lifted off its hinges in the middle of the night and stolen. Fortunately none of the horses escaped and I soon purchased another gate, painted it white and this time padlocked and chained it to its hinge pins. A couple of mornings later we found that someone had arrived in the night with what must have been a battery-powered chainsaw and neatly cut the gate into two halves, each still padlocked to the stone gate posts.

Within an hour I had joined the two halves together by screwing new spars to the two halves, slapped some white paint onto the new wood and re-hung the gate in position. The next morning all that was left were a few bits of splintered wood left chained to the gate posts and a trail of splinters and pieces up the road where the local yobs had dragged the gate – probably by a chain attached to a tractor. The situation became completely bizarre.

All these attacks were reported to the local police who claimed to have increased their patrols along the road bordering the sanctuary. Each attack was also reported by the local newspapers and one or two by local television news programmes. One morning we found that during the night someone had opened another gate and let our entire herd of horses out onto the local roads. Fortunately we found Patricia nonchalantly leading them back along the metalled road towards our main entrance, but it is not difficult to imagine the sort of carnage that could have resulted if a vehicle had driven into the horses in the narrow unlit roads near the sanctuary.

Thankfully, no-one actually attacked the animals or poisoned our reservoir or water troughs. All the attacks were concentrated on the sanctuary entrance, and when the vandals gave up attacking the actual gate itself they evolved a new tactic of regularly shot-gunning out our telephone lines.

This sort of persecution is not easy to cope with. Our actual living quarters were a couple of hundred yards down a steep track from the gate. Even if you heard a gun shot or a vehicle in the early hours of the morning, by the time you could pull on some clothes and run up the track, the vandals were long gone into the unlit country roads and lanes of the Somerset and Devon border. The battle really ground me down. Lack of sleep due to lying awake through the night waiting for the slightest sound, worrying about whether the attacks would be extended to the animals or staff, and retrieving from the gate the numerous gruesome and mutilated badgers and foxes left as 'warnings' to us, eventually drove me to spending nights wrapped in blankets, huddled against the stone wall just inside the main gate, with a loaded gun in my hands. Yes, that is what hate, fear and fatigue can do. It was stupid of course, but there is no doubt in my mind that if the vandals had turned up on any of the nights I sat there shivering in the cold wind, I would have used that gun. Fortunately for them, and even more luckily for me, no-one ever came during my long, cold vigils.

We made a few discreet local enquiries of course and established that the attackers drank at a nearby public house. The inn had a reputation as a hunters' pub and was once also a regular meeting place for badger diggers. It was also well-known for after-hours drinking. I had already been offered the assistance of a group of 'heavies' who came to Ferne for a week equipped with baseball bats, camouflage clothes and tents, and phosphorous flares. Looking back now I shudder to think of the consequences if they had caught anyone while guarding our gate in the dark, but at the time I couldn't have cared less what they did to any of our cowardly enemies.

With nothing happening all week, the three visited the inn on their last night, and threw their weight around for a while loudly forecasting great misfortune to anyone causing problems for the Ferne Animal Sanctuary. They reported back that none of the locals said a word.

Weeks went by without incident, until one day having returned to the sanctuary from Chard, I stepped out of the car to close the gate behind me. I noticed what appeared to be a few flakes of sawdust at the side of the drive.

I rubbed some between my finger and thumb and it was indeed fresh sawdust. Where could it have come from? Either side of the drive was a high bank out of which grew a beautiful avenue of magnificent beech trees – 80 to 100 feet tall. Peering around I saw some more sawdust at the top of the bank and scuff marks in the mud where someone had climbed up.

I climbed up onto the bank and found a situation which made my blood run cold. Someone had sawn almost completely through the three feet diameter of one of the beech trees and left it teetering on only three inches of wood. The cut had been smeared with mud and the sawdust disguised by being swept into the leaves and dirt. One gust of wind and the tree would have crashed right across the drive. I thought back to only two days before when a mini-bus full of handicapped children visiting the sanctuary had been briefly parked in that precise spot. I drove quickly down the drive and warned the staff of the danger; then phoned the police and started searching for a tree surgeon to take emergency action.

It was the last straw. I went to see a Chief Inspector and told him that he must put an end to the attacks on the sanctuary. He was shocked at the latest incident and was very sympathetic but said he couldn't spare officers to do anything but carry out the occasional patrol. He promised that any call from us reporting an attack would be responded to immediately but I reminded him that our location was such that by the time any of his officers responded to our telephone calls (provided the cables had not been shot out) the culprits had always escaped.

I told him that I was prepared to patrol the gate area until eleven or eleven thirty at night, but that I could not manage to be around at two or three in the morning when the local inn threw out its late night illegal drinkers. He smiled. 'I'm sure my officers would know if that sort of late night drinking was going on,' he replied patronisingly.

'Shall I give you the names of your officers who are often in the inn drinking in the early hours?' I asked him. His expression changed dramatically.

'No, say no more Mr Bryant, you can safely leave the problem in my hands. I am sure you will have no more problems,' he added.

And he was true to his word. The attacks ceased from then on.

(Apart from one when a local fox trapper sneaked into our top barn one night and cut all the strings of our barn-full of hay bales. But then he had spotted me taking his snares from the local hedgerows – fair enough, I suppose!

The action taken by the Chief Inspector was to warn the inn landlord and those of other local pubs, that anyone driving out a pub car park after the statutory drinking-up time would be breathalized. A few nights with Panda cars parked outside pubs at closing time soon had an effect. The local traditional late night social drinking came to an end and clearly someone with some clout warned our attackers to leave us alone as the attacks were not only resulting in bad publicity for the Hunt but also having a negative effect on local social lives!

Feudalism is very much alive in Britain's modern countryside. Our neighbour, Vernon Larcombe, a friendly and helpful tenant farmer, confided in me that although he was not a hunt supporter he received a postcard from his landlord whenever the Hunt would be using his land. The card included the 'request'; 'Please stop all earths.' What a nerve! Vernon was a small farmer trying to glean a living out of a few dairy cows and beef calves in a scruffy, run-down farm at the bottom of a long, rough, stony track. The fact that his landlord should expect him to find time to go round his land blocking up fox earths and badger setts so that the local hunting fraternity could gallop around on his land chasing foxes, speaks volumes about the gulf between the small tenant farmers and their 'gentleman farmer' landlords.

But it was worse than that. Vernon was a terrific neighbour for us. When we were baling hay on our fields desperately trying to get it into our barn before the expected arrival of rain, our baler broke down. Vernon sent his two strapping sons up with his own baler with instructions to them not to come home until the job was done. When our tractor became stuck in a boggy area Vernon was quickly on the scene with his machine to pull it out. I later discovered that these neighbourly acts resulted in him receiving thinly-veiled 'warnings' about being friendly to 'antis'.

Coincidentally or otherwise it wasn't long afterwards that the Milk Marketing Board suddenly informed Vernon that after decades of doing so they could no longer send their tanker down his track to collect his milk and that he would have to purchase his own mini-tanker and tow it to the main road each day for the milk to be transferred to the Board's tanker.

Knowing the power of the hunting fraternity and their friends within the agriculture service industry and livestock marketing system, I would not be the slightest surprised if this was a little punishment for being too friendly with us anti-hunt folk. The fact is Vernon was just a nice bloke. In the terrible winter of 1976-77 Vernon's beef cattle were marooned by deep snow in a field nearer to us than to him. He was not well at the time and certainly not fit enough to carry nine bales of hay a day on his back through snow drifts three and four feet deep. So we fed his cattle for him from our barn until the thaw came.

We tried to be friendly when we first arrived in the Wambrook community. We responded to a Womens' Institute newsletter in our first few months and entering into the spirit of village life by attending the local fete. I entered a couple of snaps in the photo-graphic competition and Sue, who was once a London florist, entered the contest for 'the best flower arrangement depicting a book title.' The announcement that Sue had won first prize was greeted with artificial smiles and much muttering behind hands.

We had our uses of course! When a local farmer returned to his tractor after lunch and found a snarling, vicious looking Collie had climbed into his cab and refused to come out, he rang us for help rather than risk getting bitten. Sue lassooed the dog, hauled him out of the cab, gave him a cuddle and brought him back to Ferne. He was just a frightened working dog that had run away from his farm several miles away after his owner had scolded him for making a mistake when bringing in his cows for milking. When his penitent owner arrived to collect him the dog was overjoyed.

And like any reasonable person if we saw a farm animal in trouble or a gate left open, we would always act. It was by no means rare to spot a sheep stranded on its back in a field as we drove around the local roads, or to find cows had escaped through unsecured gates. We also spent a lot of money on fencing, gates, animal feed, buckets etc. with local agricultural suppliers, but one local bigoted equine supplier ordered his checkout girl to refuse to serve us when we arrived at the till with a considerable amount of horse equipment from his shelves. 'I'm not serving you,' he snapped. 'You're anti-hunt.' He was clearly destined never to become a successful businessman – bearing in mind that only six per cent of Britain's 600,000 horses are used for hunting!

Country people are really no different from townies. Most are decent, pleasant people trying to get through their lives with the minimum of hassle, successfully raise children, enjoy a few luxuries and a couple of weeks holiday. However, in the countryside, if you upset the hunting Mafia, you may find suddenly find that all sorts of little obstacles are cluttering up your life. If you are the sort of person who is prepared to venture an opinion on bloodsports, you might find your life being wrecked. I have known of farmers whose equipment has been sabotaged, their livestock poisoned, dead foxes dumped on their doorsteps and shotguns fired outside their homes. I have known country people who have been threatened, spat at and even had explosives such as 'rook scarers' thrown through their windows – just because they have dared voice the opinion of the majority of British people that hunting and killing animals for sport should be banned. That is why so many rural residents never express their opposition to bloodsports within earshot of their neighbours despite the fact that all reputable public opinion polls reveal that the majority of country people share the townies' opposition to bloodsports.

I spent much of my boyhood in the fields of Somerset, climbing trees, and searching for newts in the ponds near my Yeovil home, or wandering around my Uncle's orchard and small-holding in Sherborne, Dorset. The pleasures of living in the countryside around farm animals and wildlife, picking berries and scrumping the odd apple, all pale into insignificance at the painful memories of maimed rabbits in gin traps, grumpy farmers with shotguns, gamekeepers' gibbet-lines, frogs killed by thugs and strewn around our local pond, and of dying baby jackdaws poked out of their nests and left to die.

As I commit my memories of seven years managing an animal sanctuary, I find the same problem. The pain of compassion for a never ending queue of abused animals, the callous nature of many in the countryside, the persecution we suffered because we cared, seem more vivid than the happy times, the hilarious moments and the joy of living in such a beautiful environment.

Now I am living in Plumstead, south east London. I can see foxes every night and often by day in our garden. I walk on Plumstead Common every day with my dog. It has a pond and ducks and an amazing variety of wild birds, as well as foxes and squirrels. I see more wildlife in Plumstead than I ever saw in my native Somerset. On Plumstead Common (saved from developers by rioting locals in the last century) you might find dog mess and litter, but you won't find anyone with a shotgun, you won't find traps and snares and you won't be told to clear off by some red-faced, tweed-coated landowner. You will find volunteers picking up the litter and you will find a smile and a cheery word from dog walkers. You will see plenty of dogs chasing sticks and balls, but you won't find a pack of them being urged to savage wild animals to death. And you won't need to worry about being trampled into the mud by four dozen sweating horses carrying people who can't find anything useful to do.

The fact is, many country people don't deserve the countryside!

Cleo and Ferdy, two orphaned fox cubs at Ferne